a slant of sun

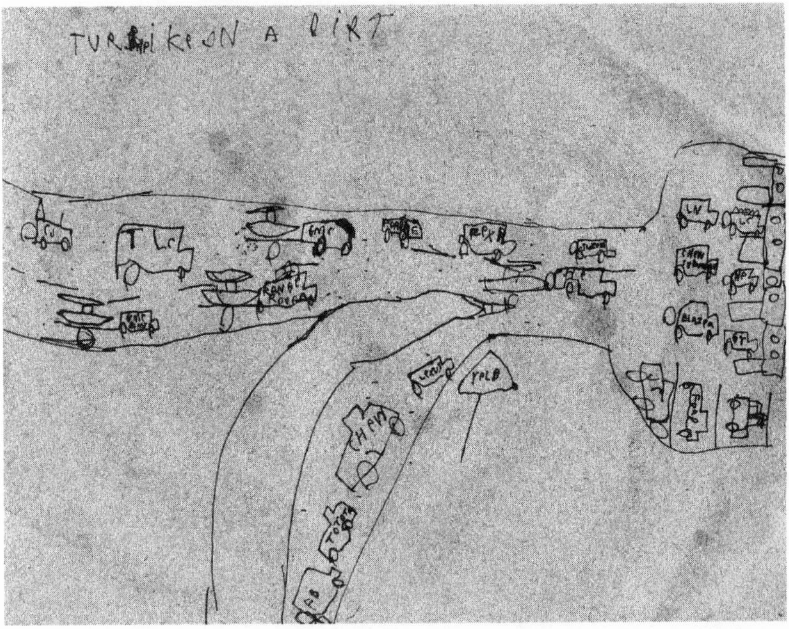

a slant of sun

ONE CHILD'S COURAGE

beth kephart

W. W. NORTON & COMPANY
NEW YORK • LONDON

Parts of this book originally appeared in different form in *Creative Reading, Iowa Woman, Iris: A Journal About Women, Northeast Corridor, Northwest Review,* and *The Sun: A Magazine of Ideas.*

Some names and identifying details of individuals mentioned in this book have been changed.

For information about permission to reproduce selections from this book, write to Permissions, W. W. Norton & Company, Inc., 500 Fifth Avenue, New York, NY 10110.

This book is composed in Walbaum
Desktop composition by Julia Druskin
Manufacturing by Quebecor Printing, Fairfield Inc.
Book design by Chris Welch

Library of Congress Cataloging-in-Publication Data

Kephart, Beth.
A slant of sun : one child's courage / Beth Kephart.
p. cm.
ISBN 0-393-02742-2
1. Developmentally disabled children—Biography. 2. Developmentally disabled children—Family Relationships. 3. Parents of exceptional children.
I. Title.
RJ135.K46   1998
618.85'88'0092—dc21
[B]   97–46973
                                           CIP

W. W. Norton & Company, Inc., 500 Fifth Avenue, New York, N.Y. 10110
http://www.wwnorton.com

W. W. Norton & Company Ltd., 10 Coptic Street, London, WC1A 1PU

3 4 5 6 7 8 9 0

For Jeremy,

who leans over my shoulder even now,

and shows me the way

contents

preface 9

dancing 15

reaching for my son 27

hat tricks 36

hard knocks 43

where silence starts 51

diagnosis 64

aftermath 77

looking for help 78

one sudden, quiet knowing 99

working it out 107

houseguest 120

waiting for the red baron 127

afternoon concert, minor keys 136

competing wisdoms 146

child's play 153

moving on 160

the farmer in the dell 174

wings 185

quaker friends 190

a slant of sun 199

from here to there 208

harm's way 217

blindsided 226

what falls away 233

palsy 242

last rights 249

acknowledgments 251

preface

*I*n the fall of 1991, Jeremy, our two-and-a-half-year-old son, was diagnosed with *pervasive developmental disorder not otherwise specified,* a confounding condition that manifested itself in Jeremy with atypical speech, impaired social interactions, a range of perseverative and compulsive behaviors, and, at times, the sorts of exceptional talents not exhibited by the ordinary child.

In truth, Jeremy's diagnosis carried the weight of the inevitable. For those keyed into the cues, Jeremy had always shown signs of being different. Music, paintings, the moon impressed him; rattles, bottles, the typical baby gear did not. He felt safe with his parents and his grandparents, but he allowed few others into his world. He was not a child who went readily from knee to knee, and by the time other children his age were waving hello, he was hiding beneath his hat or inside my skirts or far away, inside his room.

Jeremy's stance on life became even more exaggerated during his second year. If a person could survive on juice or milk alone, he would have; most solid foods were so displeasing to him that he refused to learn the basic science of a spoon. His strong personal code of likes and dislikes devolved into what, looking back, could only be fairly classified as obsessions—a violently strong passion first for trains and cars, then for hats, then knights, then planes, then trucks, the obsession with cars persisting throughout and above all the others. Though Jeremy danced with the grace of a dove and demonstrated an acute sense of balance, he was never adept at balls or tricycles, at the act of jumping or skipping, at the simplest execution of arts and crafts. And while Jeremy acquired language at a youngish age, he did not use his words as others do, did not string them together to inquire or declare. Instead Jeremy's words were deployed as epithets, affixed to those things deemed worthy of his notice.

Reflecting back, it is all too easy to identify the early warning signs, to organize them on this page. At the time, however, my vision failed me. I focused far more strenuously on my own weaknesses as a parent than on the cranks and creaks in Jeremy's development. I was a stay-at-home mother who earned my income in solitude at night by writing articles for corporations and magazines, and I was a person with a quiet life—a member of no play groups, aunt to no nieces or nephews, with a personal calendar absurdly stark and bare. I had, in other words, little to compare my son against, and so I assumed that his struggles were caused by the environment I created, my lack of expertise in the rules of mothering, and my inability to locate the proper key to his world. For a long, long time, I drew no conclusions about my son.

It took an insult from a neighborhood baby-sitter to get the message through. It took my husband, my mother, a conversation with old college friends in a motel miles from home to shatter my delusions and force me into action, into meeting with a doctor and submitting to the exams. And though it should have been helpful to have a name for the thing that was so deeply troubling Jeremy, a diagnosis is far from a cure. The fix for children like Jeremy is, I have discovered, a baffling admixture of trial and error. There is, you are told, no time to lose—neural pathways are settling in, lifelong habits are forming, behavioral tics are taking over—and so you push and push for the right concoction of language therapy, occupational therapy, play therapy, social therapy without ever having a firm sense of ultimate boundaries or goals. What, in the end, are you fighting for: Normal? Is normal possible? Can it be defined? Is it best achieved by holing up in the offices of therapists, in special classrooms, in isolated exercises, in simulating living, while everyday "normal" happens casually on the other side of the wall? And is normal superior to what the child inherently is, to what he aspires to, fights to become, every second of his day?

My husband is an artist and I am a writer, and Jeremy is the child we created. In him we saw so many aspects of ourselves—compulsivity, aloofness, strong-mindedness, anxieties—and yet the challenge we faced was to free him of our genetic code, our habits. We made up our own rules as we went along—consulting with the therapists who "felt" right, implementing our own idea of appropriateness at home, divining highly personalized theories about progress. It was a lonely business. It pushed us to our extremes. It required more of me than I actually had to give, and at the end of it all, it was Jeremy himself who provided the light and the wisdom that moved us forward.

This is a book about a little boy and his mother. It is about a child who against all odds is learning to live in this world, to even, incredibly, make it better. It is about shame, prejudice, fear, solitude, and their natural counterparts. About reaching out and holding on.

Today Jeremy, our only child, is a successful second grader at a country Quaker school. He is reading difficult books with dramatic emphasis, designing mazes for his father, whizzing around in adult computer programs, asking grown-up questions on class field trips, writing fiction in a daring hand on an oversized notepad, Rollerblading with a vengeance, shooting fourteen baskets into the hoop during gym. He goes to the parties of his Quaker classmates, and he tells me the stories of their lives: James is a musician, Eliza has a new baby sister, Meghan knows how to spell all the words in the world, Will will be an inventor when he grows up. Lately Jeremy has even been learning how to do recess, discovering games like hide-and-seek, let's-play-house, and store. And though social cues sometimes elude him, though speech can at times catch in his throat, though there are habits that still need overcoming, Jeremy, in my book, has won the battle against his genes. In the process, he has made me who I am today—gentler, more patient, more honest, more faithful, so deeply respectful of the courage of young hearts.

a slant of sun

dancing

*T*hey bring him to me just after dawn. I turn, and he is there. They show me how to bend my arms so that I can take him down toward my heart, and there is nothing else to say. The nurse leaves. I fall profoundly, madly into love, peel the aftermath of birth from my son's black-haired crown, try to slow down the shifting of his well-lashed eyes. *Hey, little guy. Over here. It's me. I'm your mom.* He is as light as that part of the dream that, come morning, slips away and slips away again. I bundle him tightly in the blankets provided and stare without comprehension at the nurses, who have now returned with instructions on the care and feeding of newborns. I don't believe that I will ever learn what they are trying to teach me, and I ask them quiet, obedient questions until my husband comes to rescue me and I can lobby for a quick release from the hospital.

Soon I'm being conveyed home in a rusting white Ford Mustang whose only defense against the persistent July heat involves my fiddling with the windows, cracking them just wide enough apart so as to whip up strong blasts of air. It is the hottest day of a long, dry summer, and Jeremy, one day into life, is blanketed and behatted in the car. His head keeps rolling around above his shoulders, though my hus-

band is driving old-man slow, and I feel criminal exposing
him to the heat and potholes like this, make him a promise
I will never keep: "Hey, after this, no more cars. We'll walk
the world."

We sleep in the same room. We lie, most of those first
nights, in the same bed, my husband and I curled like
parentheses around our son, barricades against the dark.
There is nothing to do but to feed him when he cries and
study him when he sleeps, take turns tracing the architecture of his bones. He is, for sure, a half-Latin child, so much
black hair on his head that I have to snip away the side-
burns, a delicate operation that seems to take me hours. It's
a misconception, I'm certain, but time itself has come
unscrewed. Everything is a still-life drawing; we are complete, we are immune. We sleep whenever Jeremy sleeps,
and in the intervals we make formal introductions: this is
yellow, this is the moon. My husband constructs a black-
and-white mobile and we dazzle Jeremy's vision with
bull's-eyes and swirls. When he cries, we walk up and down
the hallway reciting T. S. Eliot; he concedes to the hushing
persuasion of poetic anesthesia. It is all a held breath until
my parents, our friends, our in-laws, distant aunts, and
neighborhood children eagerly arrive and toast this child of
ours to the highest of heavens. I retreat when I can to the
back of the house and feed Jeremy until he seems satisfied.

－

AFTER THE FIRST three weeks of Jeremy's living are con-
cluded, after it is just me and my baby in the house and
there's no one watching eleven hours every day, I begin to
teach my son the only thing I know that counts: how to
stand in the pulse of a song and feel it tremble. I choose my
music carefully. I pillow Jeremy up on the antique rocking

chair, stand but a few feet from his two new eyes, and surrender to the avalanche of sound. I call it dancing. I call it
color, texture, energy, light. It is everything he'll need to
know if he's to plunge into the possibility of his life. "This
is music," I tell him at the start of every song. "And this is
how it looks to crawl inside it." I tell him that it's reasonable to catch music with your fist. I tell him that you can
wear it like a shirt. I tell him that it wasn't until I learned
the trick of song that I myself could feel halfway safe upon
our planet.

   We find our patterns. We construct scaffolding for the
days. We spend more and more time on the antique rocker,
whose story I tell Jeremy between songs. I tell him how I
found the chair in a thrift store on Main Street and carried
it all the way home. "I was nine months pregnant and out
to here," I confide. "And every few feet I plunked the damn
thing down in the middle of the walk and rocked until I
felt ready for more hoisting. You would have thought that
someone would have stopped to help, now wouldn't you?
Jeremy, wouldn't you? Or maybe passersby thought me
insane." Jeremy looks at me with his more in-focus eyes,
and I wonder what he's thinking, if he forgives my impul-
sive side, if, when he grows older, he will take me in his
stride. In the midst of staring at him intently, holding him,
loving him, I schedule time with a formal portraitist, but
the photography session does not go well; Jeremy will have
nothing to do with the bald man and his clucking tongue,
his lightning-like lens. He yawns a monstrous yawn and
falls implacably asleep. I pay the photographer for his time
and we agree that he will not return, and then I take
Jeremy out of his fancy suit and photograph him for hours
in casual tees.

JEREMY REACHES THE ten-week mark, and his head is now independent on his neck. He can look from left to right whenever he pleases, and he can try to look down and touch his toes. I check with the doctor, then I hang him from the ceiling in a Jolly Jumper that was sent down from a friend. He takes right to it. Propels himself up into the air with his toes, his fist in his mouth like a microphone, his whole body cued into the beat. I stand before him, and we're partners in dance, his head not even skimming my knee. In between songs he hangs perfectly still, waiting for his next instruction on life. "Isn't this great?" I ask him. "Don't you love rhythm?" And he throbs and he bobs and he picks up the cadence while he gnaws on his fist with his great toothless mouth.

He starts to sing, increasingly makes sense of this thing called voice—producing small, hesitating channels of sound, creaking and capsizing melodies. As the house begins to swell with his currents, we retire the elderly alarm clock in favor of his song, silence the car radio in deference to his solos, allow him greater latitude over the patterns of our days. A tornado storms into town: merciless. Yanking the paint off houses, hanging trees by their very necks, uprooting backyard tents and gardens, foiling wires and plans. Neighbors who did not know one another before are thrust into perfect friendships—thrown into the streets with candlesticks, anecdotes, laughed-off fears. From the shoulders of my husband, Jeremy watches the wet asphalt, the giddy collision of personalities, the terror of the skies giving way to an exhibition of strange and wonderful cloud forms. To the mayhem Jeremy begins to sing, knotting the fragments of the hour so tight together that when the tornado is later called back to memory, it's the songs that remain in my mind's eye, a mental picture of Jeremy sitting high in the sky calming the winds with his sweet, high humming.

And then there is the day that we board the train for the city, our first such adventure, a bit of spice. It is midday, an unpopular hour for train travel, and the only other travelers journeying with us are seven distinguished black women, all of them smartly attired, each of them bearing the unmistakable aspect of dignity on her face. Outside the train, the scene goes from pleasant to morose: neat plots of yard and well-dressed buildings shifting into sunken stoops and scrambled rooflines. The thin skin of heat in the roof of the passenger car begins to descend. The proud backs of the seven women sink low beneath its weight. But from the back of the train comes the voice of my son, plaintive and full-hearted with song. One head, crowned with a proper pillbox, turns to see. Another follows. Another, until the faces of the heat-broken, city-suited women rim about him like a rough-hewn horseshoe. Hands on the sticky orange seat back before him, legs planted firm on my lap, Jeremy sings a melody of his own making, deposits from his riverbed of verse. The women straighten, lean toward us. Their noble faces betray nostalgia. Fingers tap and encourage. The heat lifts up like a sheet in the wind. "Jeremy," I say, "look what you're doing with your song," and of course he doesn't know a thing. He's just singing to these strangers on the train.

WEEKS GO BY. Months. We celebrate Thanksgiving and Christmas. We kiss him on the forehead at twelve precisely, New Year's Eve. It is February now, and now it is March, and five days out of every seven, Jeremy and I are alone until dinner. Just Jeremy and me, his skin against my skin, his curiosity and intellect bursting. I breathe him in until my green eyes tear with the burn of too much loving. We rock in the chair. We walk through the house. We read. We fall within the thrall of music. We go outside, if the weather's fine. We make daily trips to the train station, begin to pursue long lists of distractions. If there is anything larger than the two of us, then this eludes me. Jeremy is sacred and so is this time, and I cling to it, selfish and greedy.

And yet there is, I admit, that point in the day when I lay Jeremy down for two hours. This is when he dreams—his eyes only partway shut; his fist stabbing the air; his body, a tender motor, purring. My cat slept this way, stretched out on the sill. I remember putting my hand where I thought her heart might be and understanding that it was smaller than my palm. Jeremy's sleep breaks the trance I've been in; all of a sudden I remember my deadlines. I'm a ghost-writer of sorts for corporations and magazines—an honest enough profession, strictly anonymous. No one ever sees me, I emphatically see no one, and yet now every day I'm on the phone, listening to strangers tell stories. They talk about fraud and insurance, property casualties, risk management, fire and shipwrecks. They talk about equitable solutions, ratios and calculations, sleights of hand. Words go back and forth; I write them down. Later, in the middle of the night when my half of the hemisphere is sleeping, I walk through the charcoal-colored hallways of my house, flick on my amber work lamp, and polish first drafts until they're reasonable. No one ever suspects just where the words come from, and that's fine by me; it's a living.

But things keep changing. Lately Jeremy has been completing his two-hour nap in a forty-minute interval. Or he's been falling asleep directly at noon, when all the executives I'm to interview are at lunch. Or we've returned from a driving junket and he's snoring in his car seat, and of course I can't just leave him there: a month ago, a few neighborhoods over, a baby left in the car by her mother was mauled to death by a famished raccoon. Oh God.

So the interview hour has been coming around, and I've been making a lot of excuses. Calling executives with my son in my arms, joking my way through half-cooed interviews. Sometimes I put Jeremy in his windup swing and tell the interviewee that I have just twenty minutes. I pretend that I have another standing appointment, but twenty minutes, in fact, is the time it takes for the swing gadget to unwind to perfect stillness. Other times I go to great lengths to preempt whatever plans Jeremy had in mind, exhausting him all morning so that later he'll be grateful for an afternoon siesta. This rarely works, and why should it? Eight-month-old babies can't possibly fathom the exigencies of global corporate life.

And so I find that I am coming up short on my options. Already I've taken on all the overseas work I can find—sealing the door to my office at four in the morning, then dialing London, Germany, Brussels, London again. Only occasionally does one of the interviewees stop and, with an accent, wonder: *Hey, anyhow, what time is it where you come from? Shouldn't you be in your bed?* I always pretend that I've made this one exception and that my life, on most weekdays, is normal.

I have begun thinking that maybe an extra pair of hands a single day a week would help lubricate the gears. Jeremy could work off any schedule he pleased, and I wouldn't

have to walk around gray-faced. One day only, and I would-
n't leave the house. I could hold my son when he cried for
me, and touch the silk of his head when he was sleeping. I
could do both at once—be a mother and work—if only I
could find the right person. So far the few friends who've
occasionally offered their help have distressed Jeremy
somehow, thrown him headlong toward terror until he was
back in my arms.

MY HUSBAND AND I don't like the one with the short hair
and shorter skirt. She's fifty-five years old and should know
better. We like the Korean girl, but she's in high school and
plays piano; the earliest she could get to us is five-thirty, and
that would be irrelevant unless I started working another
time zone. There are other options, but we dismiss them
summarily, and then we remember a woman we've seen;
she spends three days a week with a child a few houses
down. She's solid and pleasant and she takes good care of
things. I have always, albeit secretly, admired her.

She knocks on our door and settles into our sparse front
room, and the good impressions hold. We ask her the questions that come to mind, though in truth there aren't that
many. "Will you be good to my child?" "Will you be gentle
with him?" "Will you never usurp me, take my place?"
Nods. Nods. All around nods. "One more thing," I remember to tell the applicant, lowering my voice out of shame.
"We're not really people people, if you can understand
what I mean. We hardly go out. We haven't done much
socializing, in the proper sense of that word, since our son
was born, and so it's possible that adjustment will take time.
Will you mind if Jeremy's not immediately friendly? Not
hold it against him? He's an angel at heart." Nothing's a

problem. Anything will do. We agree on a price and plan for Monday.

And Monday comes. Before the appointed hour, I find myself all distraught with housework, all disrespectful and hysterical with lists: clean the bathroom, clean the kitchen, prepare company food, what would that be? Jeremy's crying and I know that he needs me, but I keep winding up his swinging chair. Twenty minutes, forty minutes, sixty. He must be seasick by now; I release him. Now Jeremy's in one hand and a dish towel's in the other, and I am trying to sing nice quiet songs, except Jeremy is smarter than that. He knows I'm nervous. He knows my body. The melody is a ruse. "Okay, little guy," I say. "I admit it. I've got the shakes. But how long has it been since we've had company over, and I do want everything to go just right." Jeremy looks at me through the haunted blacks of his eyes. I realize the commotion I've caused. "This is wacky," I tell him. "Mommy really is the worst." I throw the rag in the sink and take the two of us down the hallway to our rocker. We go back and forth and back and forth until we find our rhythm again. Jeremy's tensions dissipate after a while. He fits the feather of his skull under my chin. My head's lolled back by the time the sitter arrives. I can hardly remember why she's here.

Then it begins. With the armory of confidence that the sitter carries with her, she reaches both arms for Jeremy and waits for him to lean in her direction. He does not. He leans most assuredly closer in toward me, pulls my hair with his fist, and screams loudly. "Hey," I say. "Hey. Mommy's right here. Not going anywhere." I turn my back to the sitter to give Jeremy the view, but he recoils in an instant, hides in my shirt.

It's awkward. I'm mortified. I'm so glad Jeremy prefers

me. Still, I've got a sitter in my house and she's standing in my front room and it's too early to offer lunch, so I say, "Coffee?" She looks at me, decides I'm worth a second chance. She follows me and my trembling little boy down the hallway of overhead lights and fuzzy carpet.

Now I make coffee. I make it even though I'm a klutz in the kitchen, though it embarrasses me to be studied, if only slightly, by a woman who has probably mastered such trivia, could keep house, stock a refrigerator, brew a pot of coffee in her sleep. I try to make some small talk, but I'm the poorest of talents—launching into the plot of a recently read book until I realize that the sitter's fixed her stare at middle distance. "Oh well." I finally decide to hit the issue square on. "We'll all just sit together for a while and give Jeremy a chance to get his bearings."

That a while is an hour. It is two hours. It is us sitting around a paltry kitchen table until any hostess would agree: it's time for lunch. I go and get some, Jeremy strung around my neck with a vengeance while the sitter patiently waits. Several times I've tried to turn Jeremy to face our company, but he has proven himself stronger than me. He pulls at my shirt, mourns from the bottom of his soul, refuses to dig his head out of my chest, and clings.

I'm getting spooked. There are three hours left on the sitter's clock, and Jeremy's not budging. He won't eat his carrots, but he slowly agrees to juice—agrees, that is, if I hold the bottle at an angle that quashes any view of our lunchtime visitor. The sitter is now telling me stories about her children, about her grandchildren, about kids in general: none, in her experience, quite like my son. I am thinking about the work I have to do, about the trouble I've stirred up, about how rude I'm being, about the backward part of me that had this notion in the first place. *We were doing fine,* I hear the words in my head. *We were managing. We were happy. What's a lack of sleep compared to this?* Then I look at the sitter and feel a flash of empathy for her condition. "I'm sorry," I tell her. "I really am."

"You could help yourself, honey," she tells me, not unkindly. "Remember who's in charge here. You're the mother. He's the child. Go take a walk. I'll set things right. Give him to me."

It sets me reeling, puts me right on the edge of a knife. Clinging so hard to my son isn't healthy, but leaving him? I can hardly fathom it. "Go up and down the street," she suggests. "And put him in my arms. He won't get adjusted with you hovering."

I know that's true. I know she's conveying all the common sense in the world, and if I don't go, it shouts loudly: *I don't trust you.* And that's not it. I trust her, I do. She is an incredible woman. But how can I subject my son to what I know will shake him deeply? I made him a promise a while ago: *I'm not going anywhere.* And yet I do.

Down the street. Up and down, a sprinter's pacing, running outright when I hit the midsection near my house, because I can hear Jeremy howling. Half crazed with worry, I finally fly up the steps, open the door. "Listen," I report to the sitter, out of breath, "I'll pay you now. Consider it a bonus for a hard first Monday, and I'm sorry, I really am. We will get better at this. You know he's my only one." I'm pulling Jeremy out of her arms as I speak, giving her an envelope of cash, yanking the doorknob, nodding her out. "I'll call you," I say. "You know I'm sorry about this." Maybe she understands, but it doesn't matter. She is walking away and she knows she did not err; all of the trouble stemmed from us.

I'm in the rocker. I have music on. I'm easing Jeremy

back and forth, back and forth, slowing the tempo, stroking his crown; he is exhausted. He is, despite everything, nestling in toward me, shivering the anxiety out of his heart, letting his muscles go loose. His whimpers turn to sighs, and then he doesn't have a choice: he sleeps.

reaching for my son

*D*addy is his first word, and we log it into the book of life among the ultrasound and toe prints, the dark clipped curl, certificates, lists of gifts, threads, a fork, the photographs and their half-told tales: he wears his father's Batman cap, he sleeps inside his father's palms, he attends to the music that his father strums on an ancient wood guitar.

Only the heart knows what is true and early on, the moment of birth, I knew that my son preferred his father over me. Out of my own hollow chamber the child had come, and then, in the acid bath of light, he'd flailed until he'd found redemption in my husband's outreached finger. Clenched his entire fist around that bone—holding on tight and, as they say, for life, in the way that a bird conveys its strength to the sustaining limb of a tree.

It should be admitted that there are reasons enough to favor my husband. He inhabits his soul with more ease than I do mine, and time does not defeat him: there will be, he predicts, another day. Patient, he waits. An artist, he disdains calculations, expectations, routine, and he is in and out of space and language—prone to laughing, out of the blue, at a joke his brother made, not today or even last week, but decades ago, in El Salvador, at the water hole on the coffee farm beneath a cliff of yellow parrots. He paints and makes the old man young or the plaster bleed or the priest name his assassin, and when my husband makes his guitar sing, he falls deep inside old Spanish, closes his eyes, and finds himself where he wants to be: among the swollen smells of orange rinds and steamed *pupusas*, above the slow creak of a cotton hammock, near the familiar noise of the domestic help snapping spiders out of bedsheets. My husband is at home inside himself—leaving the things he can't control to the gods, and content with all the rest. It is this easiness of manner that gives those who know him strength.

I am the opposite, all celerity and hurry, approaching each day with the assailing, urgent sense that time is passing, that days are numbered, that the beasts of possibility must be unleashed. I have my father's habits, rising long before dawn, and I prowl the house the way insomniacs do, ticking tasks off in my mind, arranging incongruous responsibilities, hefting pegs into an imaginary board. Walking from room to room in the dark, I pull the drapes aside, separate the white slats of the blinds, and check the neighbors' houses for a beacon, a sign that I am not the lone vigilante of the night. Pacing the narrow, lusterless floorboards, navigating furniture and toys, abandoned coffee mugs, dust on the shelves, I make lists while others sleep, and finally I settle into my desk, a rectangle of teak on two firm trestles that moors me and saves me. There I sit before the window that I've never dressed and watch the night give in to day, the pink bursting through the Prussian blue before flattening itself into gold. I get what I can get done—magazine articles, corporate brochures, the beginning of a story or its middle—talking quietly to myself so as to muffle the other voices in my head, the impetuous, divergent alternatives: *Open the door and touch the dark. Go upstairs and sleep, risk a dream. Clean the kitchen, sort magazines, liberate closets, write a letter to your sister; you haven't spoken for too long.* No choice is the right choice. Something is always left undone. Only Jeremy in my arms, in my sight, keeps me calm. When he's asleep, I'm an unnatural fury.

I imagine that a child new to this world discerns the way of things. I imagine that my son, when he was born beneath the lights, desired stillness, wisdom, calm, patience—he knew he would need patience—and so he reached for the thing that would sustain him: a single finger, that he could clench with all his might. Jeremy found his father's hand, and my husband wore the fist just like a ring, leaned toward me that night of birth and said, "He already knows who I am." And Jeremy, who never forgets what he has finally learned, has understood this love of father and has never bent it out of place with doubt. *Where is Daddy?* my son's eyes have asked me and asked me, and I have made excuses and sometimes I have told small lies and at other moments I have said, "Everything is perfectly fine, Jeremy, because Mommy's here instead." A tactic that did not quell the crying in the beginning months, and did not brighten his outlook during any subsequent period, and did not change the fact that his first word was *Daddy, Daddy, Daddy,* and nothing else for a stretch of time.

I could forgive him, and I did. I could and I did because I understood the inclination and because there's no contravening the emotion that I have for my son. Nothing erodes it. It is not sand on a beach. It is the nuclear heart of things—hard as the rock of this earth. If I now walk the house at midnight among the tittering gossip of my obligations and fears, I also walk beneath a child's artful dreaming.

⟶

STILL, THERE ARE the days, hours, moments to account for, and because I am not Daddy, I feel an outsized pressure to perform—to compensate, at least in part, for who I am. It was easiest at the start, when the hours divided naturally into milk and diaper and rest, four-hour templates, six times a day, a rhythm to hang the moments on. But clocks become less instructive over time, and our clock soon did, and by the seventh or eighth month of Jeremy's living, the house devolved into a mother and a son and eleven hours of startling blankness, when Daddy, having boarded a weekday train for a city job, was gone.

I still rose early. I still made lists. I still sat above the scratched surface of my desk and did my job and watched the sky lose layers and contrived a plan for the day ahead, whose possibilities lay before me like spilled beads. A book from the library. A lesson on letters. A puppet show, my hands in the socks. A trip through the aisles of the second-hand stores, where you can't believe what they'll sell, and for what price. Walks, a constant, two or three a day, and in the near dark, at the end of it all, a reckless tribute to J. S. Bach or Carole King, Natalie Merchant, Bruce Springsteen, James Taylor, Victor Hugo. And when the earth turned and presented the stars before dusk, I'd schedule a trip to the moon, just Jeremy and me and the weathered front porch whooshing around in its glow. "See the clock?" I'd ask, pointing skyward. "See the cheese? See the stone? See the journey Mr. Gibbous makes upon his tight ellipse?"

⟶

BUT THE DAILY highlight—and we discovered this when Jeremy was still but a few months old—was the trip to welcome Daddy home. The train station was less than a mile from our house in the town's unpretentious heart of commerce, and after Jeremy's jangling infant neck was strong enough to command our small army, we pressed the stroller into service, Jeremy leading the way with his stockinged feet and bobbing hands. We'd roll down the street nodding smartly to the neighbors and explaining how we couldn't stop—we had a train to meet, appointments—and then, after a quick jig, we'd push in the direction of the main street, passing used everythings on the way—used cribs, used sportswear, used footballs, used jewelry, used boxes (very cheap), used furniture that the proprietors dared to call antique. The pizza house in the midst of this was named for a notorious politician, and defying all convention, a house remained among the thrifts—its drooping front porch and lawn oh so au courant with its decor of depleted appliances, headless rockers, discarded mop heads, and fishing rods.

At the major intersection, where the street of used things crossed the street we called Main, Jeremy and I wheeled a right turn and saw our destination rise before us. The bridge of rusty railroad tracks hung above the street like a dirty clothesline and to the left of that bridge stood the terminal itself, the side closest to us being the self-important side, with its long, inadequately roofed facility that housed the oily-bearded ticket master and the indoor waiting room. For a time, a fix-it man leased the other half of the narrow building, and people I know took their watches and toasters there, boasting later about the work the man had done and whispering, confidentially, that Mr. Fix-it did not work alone, but worked with the help of his son, an autistic known in those parts for flashes of brilliance. I never checked the story out. It seemed dark and cold, medieval.

Before Jeremy and I and our stroller could reach the station, we had other establishments to roll by. There was the karate shop, with its dirty glass windows and brass trophy bowls, and there was the big bike junction a few doors down, where the Harleys glowed like lamps on the opposite side of the glass. Jeremy and I, we just strolled on, cruised directly down Main toward the rusty cavern beneath the railroad bridge, where pigeons roosted and salt-colored formations grew like stalactites among the iron joints and bolts. There a steep flight of stairs offered access to the platform of homebound trains, and these are the steps that Jeremy and I would climb, me scooping him up, stroller and all, into my arms.

Three seasons of the year, we planned for early arrivals; winter, of course, was the exception. And depending on the day, we had our share of company on the platform—the homeless man in his four frayed coats, sifting through the fecund barrels of trash; the wet-nailed housewives in their boxy gray Volvos, waiting with bored faces for their men; the handful of teenagers who squatted and clunked in their military garb, twitching hand-rolled cigarettes between their fingers.

Jeremy and I were the anomaly—the only mother and infant on the platform—and we kept ourselves to ourselves, staying busy while we waited by reading the new batch of posters that had been plastered to the signboards overnight. Ringling Brothers is coming to town! Advance tickets to *Phantom!* Managed Care! Managed Care! Coming soon to a doctor near you! Pointing out the pictures and the colors and the letters to Jeremy, who refused to be distracted from the one thing he'd rolled halfway across town to see—the five-car train and the man who rode within.

If you stood on the edge of the westbound platform with your toes on the yellow safety line, you could see the train approaching from at least a mile away. You'd see the crossing lights go down at the bridgeless bend of track on the town's opposite side, and you'd catch a glimpse of the halted traffic, the particles of smoke and dust that coughed impatiently from tailpipes. You'd feel something shiver in the concrete beneath you, and then the bestial eyes of the train would appear, far away, two disks of bleeding color. "Here comes the train," I'd say unnecessarily to Jeremy, because he, having seen it too, had already gone electric, kicking both of his feet so hard that he'd inevitably lose his socks. I'd unstrap him from his stroller and sweep him close to me, and we'd watch in unison while the great gray fish floated effortlessly down the tracks, releasing the singular pitch of its song. Closer it came, closer, until the train was the only thing you could see—bigger than the signboards, bigger than the city beyond the bridge or the half-lit moon—and when it got too frighteningly close, we'd retreat, taking several big steps back until we were no longer in danger of the violent currents that the train carried forth.

All five doors of all five coaches drew apart at the very same instant, and we had to step back again to let the crowd of people through—bald men in rumpled overcoats, awkward men with fresh-cut stems, well-coiffed women in snakeskin shoes, hands in gloves, hands in hands, hands lugging briefcases, paperbacks, umbrellas, groceries, duffel bags, laundry bags, a lone suitcase or two—and Jeremy in my arms, straining, stretching to find his father's face among the other faces that poured and then trickled from that train. "He's coming," I'd promise. "Daddy's here. Do you see him?" Knowing, as I said those words, as my husband approached, as he lifted our son from my arms, that eleven hours of the day were done, eleven hours of amusements, choices, glass beads on a string—delay tactics, really, when you added them up, because the one and only great event had finally journeyed home.

⟶

JEREMY PRODUCED HIS first word when he was ten months old, and it wasn't a declaration but a question: *Daddy?* Meaning, Is Daddy home? or When is Daddy coming? and my answer, shameful as it is, was: "My name is Mommy, and aren't we having fun?" My feelings for my son were, as I have said, in no way tarnished by this exchange—it is impossible to tame the love of a child—but something inside me did go frantic, and I confess that I worked even harder to win, not preference, but favor in the bright black eyes of my elusive child. At night, I sorted the glass beads of every thinkable adventure and strung them, elaborately, into plans, and during the day I engineered trips to the zoo and its stentorian lions, drives to the city and its noble museums, escapades to the nearby pond, where we'd take our bread crusts and feed the honking, gawking ducks. We spent time in bird sanctuaries without ever spotting a bird. We walked through freshly plowed farmland with a friend. We went to the mall and bought what looked fun, and we plunged our hands through cases of Play-Doh, leaving our blobby constructions on the windowsills to dry.

But Jeremy is an independent spirit, and our excursions didn't persuade him; he always had plans of his own. Throughout the end of his first year and the beginning of his next, he let it be known, in so many words, that he preferred waiting out the hours on the small wedge of our back deck. Compliant and hoping to please, I bought a turtle sandbox and brought it home, lugged it into position on the deck, and filled it with bags of hardware-store sand. I dug tunnels and tracks like my older brother once dug, and I filled the sandbox with buckets, shovels, and bright red funnels—the machinery of child labor. I took a chair outside and a book, and the last thing I did was carry Jeremy to the stuffed green turtle, opening the cranky back door and, in a parody of drumrolls and horns, announcing magic. "Okay, you rascal, here it is, the very thing that you've been waiting for," I told him, and Jeremy, I'm almost sure, smiled a small smile, then tripped into the sandbox and collapsed upon my tunnels.

It was hot. I read. I let him be. He used the tools not to construct, as I'd anticipated, but to meticulously drain the turtle of its clean white crystals, dumping cupfuls and spoonfuls of sand out of the box onto the deck, watching it slide away between the cracks in the wood floor—fascinated, curious, perhaps even content. It was hot, and I read, and he played. It was hot, an eleven-hour day, and Jeremy and I ate lunch outside, and we shared snacks outside, and every half hour, the railroad tracks that ran behind our yard would scorch and rattle with the promise of an incoming train. "Daddy!" Jeremy would point. "Daddy!" he would stand up and exclaim as the train swished by, and I—wary and exhausted, acquiescent, unsure—would look up and consider, then offer the best reassurance that I could. "That was a one-car train, Jeremy," I'd tell him. Or, "That train, an Amtrak, was red and blue." Or, "Daddy loves you, little guy. I promise you. He's coming home."

hat tricks

*I*t starts with rain: drops, buckets, days of it, so much rain I think my very porch might sink or my pine trees sail or my neighbor's cat die all nine lives by drowning. It starts with rain, gallons of rain, and the way such things move through young boys and their moms.

"What will we do?" I ask my son, for by now we can work the puzzles blind and tell the stories backwards and run every match-car race in the book.

"Hats," says Jeremy. At least that's what I think he says.

"Hats?" I ask. (He's not yet two, I want to be sure.)

"Hats," Jeremy nods confidently.

"Get your shoes and your coat and we're off," I say, but I hardly know where and for what purpose.

Behind the wheel of the car, I drive nowhere thinking about hats. Hats? I wonder. Hats? Where can we go to find hats? And then it comes to me like a spear of lightning—a marvelous memory of hats. "I have an idea," I call out to Jeremy, all strapped in behind me. "I know a place that is swimming with hats," I say, and I steer the car toward a department store several miles off.

We arrive and we do not dawdle in the store; we march

straight over there, to the hats. I count six hat trees, each tree with a dozen branches, each branch sprouting two leaves, the leaves being, of course, the hats. In the corner, near the cash register, is a full-length mirror in front of which to try the fashions on.

Maybe we spend an hour here. Maybe we try four dozen hats. We move from berets (every imaginable hue) to caps (both plaids and solids) to the high-society affair, with broad rims and flowers and bows. We are in the very last grove, in the felts and fedoras, when my son finds the hat of his dreams.

Perhaps I should say up front that Jeremy favors green. He likes green bright as a grape, green dull as an olive, green calm as an overcooked pea. Today, the breed of green on his mind is chartreuse, and when he finds it he will not turn back.

"Hat," he tells me assuredly, looking very much like a green umbrella.

"How about the red cap?" I tell him, squirming. "How about the yellow-and-blue-striped straw?"

"Hat." Jeremy puts both hands to his head and presses firmly, as if some wind is about to separate him from his find.

I look and I consider. We are speaking, now, of an over-sized fedora-style ladies' hat—dull crease separating cavity from rim, a thin strip of black velvet running ragged all the way around the wide perimeter. A hat coming so far down on my child's head that the first available organ is his nose. On all the trees, on all the branches, among all those dozens of leaves, there could not be a more controversial choice.

"I'm not sure about this one, Jeremy," I say, imagining my husband's reaction. "Let's look again."

"HAT," Jeremy says, as if I hadn't heard him the first time.

All the way home in the car, Jeremy, delighted, kicks the back of my seat.

⟶

JEREMY AND I are rinsing spinach at the kitchen sink when I hear my husband's keys in the door. I know he's out there on the porch, struggling with his shoes, flapping the umbrella dry, stripping himself of his coat. My mind goes off at racing speed—fashioning defenses, excuses, small lies. It was an accident, I think I'll say—a gift, a hand-me-down—but before I get any of my tales sufficiently straight, my husband is guessing the truth.

"What is that?" he asks, leaning toward his son and tapping the felt. "Anybody home?" And then to me, above the green, he uses his lips to spell R-E-T-U-R-N.

"Hat," Jeremy answers, putting his hands to his head and pushing the felt piece up so he can see.

"The kind they leave on benches at bus terminals," my husband grumbles.

"I know," I say with what I'm sure is a grimace. "But he likes it."

"Okay, I suppose that's fine," my husband says, after what seemed like a pretty long time. "So long as he doesn't wear it outside, I suppose we should say that that's fine."

Jeremy eats dinner with his green hat on. He takes a bath in it. He takes it to bed and sleeps in its creases. When he wakes up in the morning and comes to our room, the word that he says is *Hat.* The writing is on the wall; even if my husband and I don't say so, we know.

⟶

TODAY, A MIRACLE: the sun. I do not argue when Jeremy, behatted, turns the front-door knob and strides his five-inch-long feet across the porch. I do not say, *Please reconsider.* I do not present a point of view, an alternative, a warning. No, despite the fears I harbor in me, the hat is down the steps and onto the sidewalk before I turn the key.

What kind of mother lets her son parade in an oversized piece of chartreuse? What woman would not, out of kindest motivation, protest and insist: *But you can barely see!* What mother knows so little of gender and style, fashion and fit that she will not thrust upon her son a big ten-gallon or the pinstriped colors of the local team? He's not even two; can it matter? I comfort myself with the hope it does not.

We walk all of twenty feet before we meet our first resistance: our neighbor with the cat, the big-hearted man who's famous for fixing anything. "Hat on the wrong head?" he asks jauntily from under the hood of his car, where he's working.

I lie and tell him yes. "It's just a loaner," I call out, cheery. And quicken my pace, and blush.

"You are definitely in a phase," sings out another neighbor (several houses down), in a voice she assumes is placating. "Not to worry. He'll be over this in no time. Worse cases have been solved!"

At the corner deli, one elderly clientele mistakes my son for a daughter. The checkout clerk offers empathy; the bag boy, with all the wisdom of his sixteen years, says (not cruelly), "My bet is he'll lose that green thing by tomorrow."

～

WE ARE SPEAKING now of several tomorrows, dozens of them stacked up tall, each against the other. Save for the thirty-second shirt change in the morning and the bath and pajamas again at night, the hat is a fixture on my child's head. That is to say he also sleeps in it, preferring it to stuffed toys, not minding at all the wide creases that grow up all over the felt like lines on a relief map, or the gradual shedding of the black velvet hair. We begin to call it the Paddington with ample cause. Our polite requests for a hat reprieve go spectacularly unheeded. "Do you want to give your head a rest?" we ask. Jeremy places both hands on his head and vehemently shakes his head, and that, we quickly understand, is all there is to that.

Outside we remain the subject of much notice, and I begin to amuse myself by cataloging the stares. The *did you ever* is by far the most popular brand—a reaction that cuts across age, gender, class, and (I'm sure) religious affiliation. Running neck and neck for second are the *proud to know you's* and the *ain't no way to raise a man's man*—the former typically emanating from a striking assortment of long-haired teenage boys, ladies with kind, far-seeing eyes, and men and women with their own sense of fashion; the latter sort of look cast off, mostly, by muscular men in sleeveless ribbed shirts. Jeremy's hat stops lovers from kissing, starts truck drivers hee-hawing, detours conversations, even swings moods. I watch all this; I take notice.

We acquire a reputation. We become (how should I say it?) *known*. We emerge as the protagonists in other people's tales, collect stories of our own. One day, we make a left-hand turn into a neighborhood party store—a place we have frequently seen but never entered. We are there for balloons, a bright bouquet of them (a whim), and when we go to the counter with our colors in mind, we are greeted by a pleasant little screech. "Maria," the balloon lady calls to someone in the back, "MARIA." A pause, a giggle: "HE'S HERE, Maria. THE BOY WITH THE GREEN HAT IS HERE."

I turn. From behind a veil of wooden beads, I see a pretty, dark-skinned woman dropping whatever it is to the floor and pushing her way to the front. "OH!" she cries out to Jeremy in some kind of wonderful accent. "OH. You have come in. You visit us. I'm so pleased. So pleased. I've seen you passing every day, and I have wanted—such a long time I have wanted—to say hello to the boy with the hat. Here," she says, grabbing a balloon from the bin and pumping the thing up with helium. "Here: a balloon on the house. A green one, for your hat."

At the train station, recently, we were stopped in mid-waiting by a lady of no more than thirty. "I love your boy's hat," she told me, standing quite close and looking urgent. "I watch out for it every day. A beacon of sorts," she said, "the sign of a spirit set free." And then she waved, and the train crowd was pressing in, and before I could think of what to say, she was gone.

Not all the stories are as wise, or as fine. Only last week, at the playground, there were boys—five of them, kindergarten-age. "Look at that hat." They slurred the words in loud disapproval. "Look at that sissy hat. He can't play here, not with us, until he takes it off." They stared right at me and said it, as if I would take their side. They locked arms and stood, miniature warriors, holding their ground.

Jeremy's not big enough to understand, or perhaps he is. I led him quietly away, I wanted to explain, I wondered. I thought about the future. I thought about the pressures from all sides, the claims and the disclaimers, the praise and the jeers that accompany any decision that is truly one's own. Today it is a chartreuse hat with an ebbed-out crease and rain spots buried in the brim. Tomorrow it will be an idea, a profession, a cause.

"Set your kite high," I told him softly, going home from the swings, "and clench your fist tight around the string. And hold on, hold on."

hard knocks

A few months before Jeremy turns two, we hear about a writer who is renting her Victoriana home in midcoast Maine for the summer season. It sounds just right. We're told we can get it cheaper if we reserve the last two weeks of May, and that sounds right, too; it's official. One Friday my husband comes home early from work. Everything is packed and by the door. The only thing left is to heft the luggage into the car and get Jeremy settled into his back-seat car throne.

Outside there's the spirit of summer in the air; the sky is a clean blue color. The neighborhood kids have started bursting from their homes, threading up the street on bikes and boards, convening in the block's essential center, which is just half a house west. It's ragtag and festive—the scooters and the jump ropes the kids drag out with them, the shirttails that flap in the breeze, the ponytails that bob high on the heads of little blond girls and little brunettes—and now the youngest ones are bringing up the rear on tricycles with plastic streamers. One pushes a doll carriage; one stumbles behind a bug-faced walker whose eyes are rolling around in its head. In either direction mothers stand on porches watching or they wave to one another; some straggle up the street toward the knot that is now forming. No master plan is in the wind; kids pair off in twos, then threes, play on the fringes of the undecided mass until the entire congregation parks itself on the lawn of the house across the street. It's a flat lawn, and it's already staged with a main attraction. A wooden post with its foot in the ground. A ball tethered on a string.

The commotion has its irrefutable lure, and Jeremy, who rarely exhibits interest in the neighborhood drama, is watching alertly from the porch. We are sitting together on the splintered floorboards, and Jeremy is newly hatless, chapeaus having suddenly lost their attraction a few weeks ago. Inside, my husband prepares the house for our absence and studies the map one last time. "Look at all those kids, Rascal," I whisper to Jeremy. "Can you believe they actually fit inside the houses on this street?"

Jeremy doesn't necessarily answer me, but he throws his capped juice cup down in a demonstration of radical enthusiasm and repeats, *Can you believe they actually fit inside the houses on this street?* "You little rascal," I say. *You little rascal,* he echoes back. When the neighbors to our immediate left make an appearance, Jeremy uncharacteristically decides to clop down the steps and join the crowd. I walk him to the edge of the sidewalk, check for cars, then let him go. Stand there, just like any other mom. "Be careful," I caution. *Careful.*

I nod a hello to the next-door neighbor who has inspired this streak of courage in my son. It is the one family on the street for which Jeremy has shown any continuing affection—traipsing over to their sandbox occasionally, paying attention to the antics of the youngest boy. It's not that Jeremy actually plays with this boy—and who would expect that, neither one is yet two—but he does admire him, doesn't mind, from time to time, plopping down in his company, sharing a room. Sometimes I think that it's the mother who's the draw, a French Canadian Christian woman who makes Jeremy feel at home—doesn't get huffy or thrown out of joint when Jeremy walks by without a greeting, doesn't give me that *I'm insulted* attitude when he won't look in her eyes. Jeremy's not big on hellos just yet, he doesn't see the value of looking someone in the eyes. My neighbor understands that every one of us is different, and Jeremy senses her goodness, likes her company, and so do I. This is the woman who delivered cinnamon rolls on our first day in town, then thought to make a second delivery: a knife, some butter. This is the one who shared her children with me before I was pregnant with my son—who sent them knocking on my front door with the news, the proof of a missing tooth; let me photograph them all costumed for dance rehearsals; said it would be all right if I treated them to a roasting fire, the marshmallows that go with it. This is the woman who has steadfastly read my poor attempts at poetry and then rendered her reactions in exquisite and insightful prose, leaving the letters in the box outside my door so as not to disturb the mothering rhythms I'm in. For me, increasingly, she is the world outside family, keeping me just this side of lonely.

But Jeremy's been inclined to spend more and more time alone in the house, been decreasingly interested in people, and so I've been seeing less of her, am grateful for this unexpected moment when Jeremy joins the cavalcade of kids and when she, like me, takes up her station on the walk. We edge closer to each other and start our conversation wherever the last one had left off, and first I am watching Jeremy while talking to her, then I am looking at her because she is making me laugh, and it feels so good, this great abandon. Every once in a while I check in across the street, and note that Jeremy's there in the circle of kids watching some of the older boys devise a game with the tethered ball. My husband has started lugging the suitcases to the car. The door slams and creaks open, slams again.

It's a beautiful evening, reminds me of lost summer nights when my brother and I would sit beneath a crest of brightening stars, watch the stubby bats swoop low, and listen to the kids next door, my mother washing dishes. Familiar, calming, anchoring sounds that suggested that life itself is inexpugnable. Right now, this moment, I feel that way, with my son across the street and my neighbor at my side and my husband in the house getting ready for Maine. Things, I think, are pretty good. I'm kidding my neighbor about my upcoming trip; we anticipate the books I might find in the absent writer's house.

Suddenly, it goes off like a siren—one note gaining in density until I realize that the sound is my son. I jerk my eyes across the street and don't see him, see other kids bent at the waist. Kids leaning over something on the ground, something wearing Jeremy's shoes; my neighbor and I start running at the same time. By the time I get across the street, Jeremy's upright again, holding his head, eyes all black liquid, a look of shock. "Tell me what happened," I start demanding of the others, accusing before I know the facts. "Did somebody push him? Somebody hit him? Why is he crying? Somebody tell me." He's in my arms, I hold him tight as I can, start stroking his hair, find the lump on his head. "How did he get this?" I'm almost crying. "My God, he only came out here to play." Now, to Jeremy, "I'm sorry, I'm sorry. This is my fault. I wasn't watching. Are you okay?"

But obviously Jeremy's not okay, and what I gather from

the kids is that someone smacked him with the ball. "We hit the ball with a bat, see? And Jeremy was standing right there and got knocked over. He was just standing there. It was like he wasn't watching. Like he didn't see what was coming. It wasn't our fault. He was just standing there when it happened." I'm getting all this and trying to process it when my husband comes up beside me, pulls Jeremy from my arms, asks for answers. I say, "I just don't know."

"What do you mean you don't know?"

"I didn't see it."

"You weren't watching?"

"I didn't see it. I was talking. I'm really sorry."

"He's just a little kid, Beth. He's supposed to be protected."

"I was talking."

"Talking's so important? He's got a lump the size of a goose egg. Feel this. It's got to hurt like hell."

"I know it hurts. I know it's awful. I didn't mean for it to happen."

In my husband's arms Jeremy starts growing calmer. We cross the street. I hang my head. I signal a quick, shrinking good-bye to my neighbor. The car is packed, my husband heads right for it. I climb into the passenger's side and wait while he tends to Jeremy in the back. He runs into the house, gets some ice, fits it onto Jeremy's head. I am useless and immobile in the car.

WE DRIVE, THEN, in silence, head up to midcoast Maine. The sky turns the color of the bits in Etch-A-Sketch; eventually we put on some music. I keep turning around to tell Jeremy I'm sorry, but I'm afraid to raise the sore subject again. I look at him quietly, this progeny of heaven. His alabaster skin, his onyx eyes. He remains in that zone between alertness and sleep for what turns out to be hours. He won't look at me. He's in his own world. Not until we're on a roadway looping Boston is he finally wherever he goes when he dreams.

The later it gets, the more abandonment we feel: it is possible to leave the anger behind. To begin to exchange gossip about the truckers beside us or to fantasize about the house awaiting us in Round Pond. At one point—4:00 A.M.—we're out of gas and driving secondary roadways until we find the only place with a light on for miles. We are so relieved to get gas in the car that we clean the attendant out of his few candy bars and pass them all around. Jeremy is awake again, so we watch the sun come up— together, as a family. The lump on his head is almost gone.

Under the red eye of a brazen morning, we drive along Route 1—past Portland, Freeport, Brunswick, Bath, and Wiscasset; past unshaven landscapes, sapphire waterways, bright-colored seacraft, antique pickup trucks. Soon we are where we're supposed to be. We settle in. We take a walk. It's a town of gentle histories: a two-engine fire station, a white church, a brown church, a bed-and-breakfast, the Granite Hall Store, whose old-fashioned sign promises penny candy, Irish woolens, hand-dipped ice cream, toys. A string of honest-looking houses are dropped like pebbles along this coastal fishing village, and finally there's the harbor, a true-to-life working dock whose boats, I notice, are named like boats, not poodles, and whose boatmen work the sea. The lobster men are already out on the dock, dishing out conversation like chowder.

THERE IS A hush around the next ten days. We are plan-
less, sleeping late, impostors in the wicker chairs of our
invisible hostess, who has left a few notes around the house:
*Flush only when you must. Consider the life span of this
lightbulb.* We move around the bare blond-wood floors,
peruse the books on the low white shelves, stare out the
window into the windows of our nearest neighbor, where
what appears very much to be a child standing guard is just,
we realize later, a disheveled doll. Jeremy plays in the
morning, organizing a slow parade of fire trucks. Over and
over, the same trucks in the same sequence, admiring his
work like great art. We admire it too and try to distract
him, but he is soundlessly content with his red metal.

For lunch we by and large have lobster. We can get it so
cheap at the dock and it's fun to walk there, hand in hand
in hand, Jeremy in the middle between us, long sleeves on,
no real agenda of his own until we near the firehouse.
That's when his black eyes smolder like hot coals, when he
runs—determined, his head down—in a sure direction,
and of course we indulge his habit. "Fire trucks, fire trucks,
fire trucks," he says. "Why do you like them so much?" I
ask him. *Why do you like them?* he repeats, coy and delighted. I roll my eyes teasingly and don't press for a real answer,
for he's peaceful and happy, and we all feel whole. We shop
in the Granite Hall Store after lunch, buying out the stock
of fire trucks, one by one.

And of course we drive when we want to, find the granite cliffs and the stone-drum forts of Pemaquid; shop the
antique stores of Damariscotta; go up and down the streets
of Wiscasset. We take a day trip to Bath, head off, with our
map, in a tangle of directions—to Monhegan Island,
Portland, Camden, a string of pottery studios known as
Edgecomb. We don't talk when we drive; we listen to local

music, or we study the road signs and giggle. We encourage Jeremy to point out the things that he knows and is willing and able to label. But he's silent most of the time, except when a fire truck flies by. That's when he grows most excited. He seems to have a sixth sense, can hear them coming from miles away, even when the siren's off and they're not making more than an ordinary rumble.

The last day in Maine, we return to the Pemaquid coast, spot a red fox in the woods, walk the coarse, sandy beach, climb granite walls. On this day, we encounter few others. Right near the tip of this town stands a nineteenth-century lighthouse, and from the lighthouse toward the sea extends a long, veiny hand of charcoal-colored rock, which is etched with ocean currents and bears as well the smooth remains of broken tree limbs and shells. We scurry up and down and stare out upon the horizon, the sea winds flapping the hair on our heads and limning us slightly with salt. We separate and come together, separate and stand. The sun will be setting soon, and we know that the real world will thrust itself on us tomorrow, or the next day, when we return to our house and whatever new passions Jeremy will find there, a crate of fire trucks in tow.

where silence starts

*A*t three months or four, Jeremy did not just bounce in that Jolly Jumper; he danced, he danced resolutely. By ten months, he was uncanny and graceful—sidestepping all those doorknobs and dangers that I for sure would not have seen. By Jeremy's first birthday, he was well into his collection of words, was noisily stockpiling *juice cup, Dino, bathtub, button, yellow moon-a, yellow sun,* and applying them, anthropologically, to the commodities of his world. His words were singular—exclamations, not sentences— but they were said with such conviction and syllabic clarity that they lodged in my own mind like stories. I thought we were talking then. I want to think we're talking now. Want to believe that when Jeremy stares at length at the pictures in books, at the fire trucks and, increasingly, at the cars on the floor, at the mix of light radiating in through the window—it's poetry he's thinking about. Something too resplendent to share. But maybe I can't think that way much longer. Maybe it is time to take a half step back and see.

Home from Maine now, the heat of summer upon us, and something, I sense it acutely, is wrong. There is an absence of things. Small lights burning out. The creep of an indecipherable dimness. Jeremy does not wave hello. Jeremy does not eat his food. Jeremy does not look for us beneath the hood of his eyes; language is disappearing. Jeremy is scared to death, but where are the monsters, and why do they chase him, and who let them into this house? I lock the doors. I seal the windows. I sequester myself in my own concerns, and the house leans into itself like an abstraction.

The hats, the cars, the fire engines were all signs I should have read, but I was thinking about predilections, not obsessions. Before that, I should have questioned the rigor that Jeremy demanded—the careful patterning of toys on the rug beside his bed. I should have wondered if his shyness was more than mere shyness, his disinterest in food more than a passing phase, his unwillingness to look a cherished neighbor in the eye more than a bad habit he'd acquired, his lack of inquiries, questions, declarations somehow more telling than I had been allowing. I should have stopped—once, twice—to hear the way he'd started speaking. To catch the echo and observe it, intuit a larger implication. "Do you want to go to bed?" *Do you want to go to bed?* "Can you give me a big kiss?" *Give me a kiss?* "Are you happy?" Silence. Silence.

IMAGINING MOTHERHOOD IS like imagining yourself old: there are no accurate forecasts. I guess I assumed I would know more. Pregnant, I supposed that mother's intuition was a hard, certain thing, a perpetually replenishing reservoir of basic instinct. If there were problems, the gut would howl it. If there were risks, the heart would rattle. If the jumbled trivia of daily existence pulled into and into itself like a knot, the mother's hands would separate the strands. But it has not been that way for me. If there is a road map here, some compass inscribed in my soul, I have not found it. Every day since the first one with Jeremy has been a mystery. I am no wiser, or any less vulnerable, for having given birth to a son.

I recognize that mine is a less than universal situation. During Jeremy's first two years—out in the world, at the grocery store, in the park—I heard how other mothers spoke to their children: firm, decisive, self-confident. *You have had too many cookies. You are not behaving well. Hurry up! We're out of time! We will not buy this or that and you will stop eating that chocolate because I am your mother and I know what's healthy for you.* I admired those mothers for their fast list of facts, for the way they could pull out their opinions like a pen and mark them down. I wondered at the unequivocal quality of their instructions, their encyclopedic knowledge of right and wrong. I felt inadequate, permeable, without conviction. I took my son's side in the arguments we might have been having. I introduced him to chocolate, that secret pleasure. I gave him time because it gave me time to watch his Latin features settle deeply on his face. We were alone together, day after day, and there were no rules, no map.

Increasingly, Jeremy wasn't asking for much; it seemed that I had been let off the hook. At the stores, he did not point and insist. In the stroller, on the porch, he watched the sky—intently, passionately, a readerly pose. At home, he had no favorite food he battled for, no TV habit to discourage, no whining demand that we play this game or that. I could have left him alone for hours with his cars; he was that self-contained. The Fords, the Chevys, the MGs, the old Rolls-Royces were spectacular creatures in glimmered chromes—crimson, midnight, teal, lipstick red—and he would lie on the floor and bring them in close and rock them, back and forth, on the rug. Then he would park them in mathematical pinwheels, and nothing could be changed after that. Not if we wanted to preserve the peace in the house. Not unless we had the strength of spine to let him cry for hours, such a terrible sadness, and not conclude that it was best to just give in. We began to move with meticulous care around his artlike constructions, felt the house slowly freezing into place. I remember thinking that I was suddenly much too tall and much too thin to be a mother, and that no amount of stooping could bring me into my son's space.

It seems to me that my inability to enter my son's world is a personal failure, a crisis. I do not mention it to the few friends who call. I hide it from my family, and I decline to talk about such things with my husband, who somehow always understands where Jeremy's cars are going and why; knows, just by observing, which car is the odd car out and free for moving. I can't talk to my husband because he is the better parent, and so in the dark at night, I lie awake and wonder, worry about the instincts I am lacking, and conclude—horrified—that love alone may not be enough.

In an awkward attempt to somehow make contact, I begin to rearrange things in my house. Though it is cars that Jeremy adamantly admires, I start insisting upon books. Though he craves solitude, we spend increasing hours with the boy next door, his bright balls, his predictable mix of boy things. Though order is sacrosanct, I tip the balance of things, put this Ferrari there, that Model T on the shelf, a clutch of white flowers on the sill among the hats. I am simply trying to move him out of his world into mine, to find a common ground.

It isn't working. Jeremy makes it clear that he could not care less about storybooks—looks out the window while I read, strains to get back down to the floor, where his priceless cars are waiting. He likes the backyard of our friends next door, certainly trusts the mother and son, but play at my neighbor's house becomes very much like play at home; Jeremy finds the cardboard box of cars and lines them up in a row, leaving the other child to his own devices. He grows less inclined to let people in the door, minds the mailman, even, prefers the playground in its early empty hours.

What can I conclude but that perhaps it is time for Jeremy to spend time away from home—get some distance, make his own friends, have a chance to respond to someone else's mix of ideas. There is a woman. I met her by accident. She has a daughter, a house, two other young charges, a garden of carrots, yarrow, pachysandra. She seems at ease with herself, perfectly confident in her ability to mother. She has it all worked out, and she tells me what she knows when I encounter her in all the neighborhood places. Tells me about obedience, respect, fun, a child's mind. Tells me she's never flustered; she's in charge. After several chance encounters and a formal meeting in her home, we agree that Jeremy will spend five hours a week in her care. We lay out, very carefully, what he will do there, how she will treat him, how she will attend to his quiet, how much it's worth. Though it is unspeakably painful for me to prepare the groundwork for separation, I believe I am doing what is best.

IT IS THE middle of August. Jeremy has just turned two. Outside, the air is wet as steam, and above me Jeremy lies transfixed and unsuspecting with his cars while I pack his stroller with everything he will need. At nine-thirty, I climb the stairs, walk down the low-ceilinged hallway, and push back the door to his room. Call his name, but he doesn't look up. Say, "Jeremy, hey, Jeremy," move toward him, bend down, turn his face toward mine, pull him away. He comes unwillingly, heavy in my arms, one hand still curled around a miniature old-fashioned milk car, the other hand empty. He wails, a wordless protest. "We're going to go make some new friends," I tell him, though he isn't asking questions.

The houses in my neighborhood stand perilously close to one another, and they are perched right near the street, some with stone porches, some with the roofs toppling down, some with junkers in the backyards instead of swings, some recently done up, like beauty-parlor queens. Children are everywhere, here on the streets, boisterous and mostly well cared for, normal in every sense of that word. The mothers who don't work cluster on stoops, engage in ragged conversation. Fathers drive their second-hand cars to work. It's got an old-fashioned feel, a casual quality that is easy to blend into, but today, carrying Jeremy through the front door to the waiting stroller, taking the blows of the milk car on my shoulder, my chin, unable to quell the noise of his anger, I feel like an interloper, shattering the calm. Fighting the stroller, fighting its seat belt, fighting me, Jeremy hollers his anger down the long line of that street. I walk behind him, saying words he refuses to hear.

The sitter lives a few blocks away—on the other side of the train tracks, past the brown-brick warehouse of party supplies, past a faceless manufacturer of steel bolts and fasteners. The quickest route to her house involves a diagonal swath through the community park, a big expanse of green that has a dusty baseball diamond at its core and two splintering benches, sited perpendicularly, on either side of the home-plate fence. In August at this time of day, the park tends to be empty, save for the swarm of striped bees at each trash can and the conspiracy of mosquitoes near the trickle of the creek. By the time Jeremy and I reach the park, his screams have softened into a sobbing, languageless disbelief, and hoping he can hear me now, I talk. I tell him everything, say I'm not sure I'm doing all things right by him, as his mother. Maybe I love him too much. Maybe love is an excuse; I don't know. "I'm taking you to a new friend," I say, "and there will be new toys there, better food, a new routine. You won't have to bore yourself silly with those cars. Give me that milk car, Jeremy. Uncurl your fingers. Show that you trust me, at least trust me that much."

At the sitter's I stay more than an hour with Jeremy, standing by so that he can settle in. There are three other children in the house, and they all seem shockingly mature, verbal, direct, fully opinionated on topics I don't have the first sense of right or wrong about. There is hierarchy in their play: the boy as the ordained leader, the youngest child alternatively mascot and dud, the girl in the middle, between the boys, flirting and appeasing, screaming angriest of all whenever the balance of play is overturned. The sitter has a small, well-kept, straight-out-of-a-magazine-full-of-florals house, and there aren't any hallways, just rooms, so that it is easy to see from one space to another, to watch the older children as they chase between the kitchen and the toys, around the dining room table, now stick wood ponies between their legs as they gallop in delight and then

fury. The sitter is at the sink scraping carrots for a snack. I
sit down on her family-room couch. The milk car still in his
hand, Jeremy is running a confused and anxious circle
before me—ignoring the other children, taking no interest
in the pine chest of rattles, puzzles, plastic books, army
trucks, the requisite doll or two for the girl. "This will be
fun," I tell him. "The other kids want you to play with
them. Look."

I stay too long, whispering false encouragement to my
son: "The boy is playing with dump trucks, go see. Can you
show the baby this plastic book?"

"He'll do better without you," I'm warned by the sitter.

"I'm out of here," I say. I hold out my hands to extract
Jeremy from his circle. I kiss him, some kind of a promise,
on his cheek. "When I come back," I tell him, "I want to
hear about the fun I know you'll have."

I hear Jeremy cry as I turn the knob on the sitter's door.
I hear him cry as I descend the six cement steps. Hear him
through the tomato hedge, through the metal gate, into the
field, into the diamond. Hear him when by all rights I
should only be hearing the bees, their electric noise and
panic in the hollow of old beer cans.

➤

Twice a week, for two terrible months, Jeremy and I
make our way to the sitter. Me packing his things, climbing
the steps, saying his name, standing above the sphere of his
play in violation of ranks and patterns, until his body closes like a fist and his eyes refuse mine and his whole self
declaims against the destination that he now anticipates
and rues. Once outside, I strap him, bucking, into the
stroller, and we push through the heat and past the gaze of
the casual women on stoops who have learned to wait until

we pass by to continue their gossip. At the sitter's house, I stay—urging, confounded, not hopeful—while she dices celery at the sink and her daughter leads a parade and Jeremy races in circles at my feet, drilling a wedge into the carpet. Later, it is my heart chasing me as I run home, out the gate, through the park, across the train tracks, past the women—the vacant sound of my own betrayal in the scolding August air.

At home at night, my husband and I speak in terms of adjustment, natural reactions to unforeseen circumstance. We weigh Jeremy's terror against Jeremy's solitude, his habits, his lying dead still on the floor of his bedroom. We hide our anxieties from each other, draw conclusions, decide singly and together that it is best to give this time. A clean house. Organic food. Children. Isn't this what Jeremy needs? Doesn't he need a change of view, a new agenda, new possibilities? Increasingly, I am not sure, but I don't feel like I have an alternative: I push on. Through August and September, into early October, I read Jeremy's solitude and rage, his desperate circles, his empty gazing at the sun, his indifference to sleep or food as barometers not of an inherent disability but of my own inability to mother. They are the consequence of a woman without a map, a parent who has fallen so deeply in love with her son that she has kept him from the world for too long and now lacks the grace to pull him back into it. It is my fault, and I ask no one, save Jeremy, what to do.

Though now and then the sitter offers her opinion. It's not solicited and I have to say that it isn't welcome, don't know if it's even civilized—the things she says, the way she says them, when we are standing on her front stoop, the children inside. In the self-confident way that untroubled people can have of speaking, she reports on movies she's seen, recent cinematic releases like *Rain Man*. "Oh my God," she says, rolling her eyes. "Imagine giving birth to a Rain Man." In full-blown detail she describes a cousin she grew up with, someone older than she, who was retarded. "He was disgusting," she says, just like that, no ounce of mercy, and then, as if I deserve the benefit of her thinking, she tells me of a pledge she made with her husband. "Ever we had a messed-up kid, we'd put him in an institution, let him be somebody else's problem, not ours," she says. "You get but one life to live and you can't waste it spooning oatmeal into a half-brain. We're so happy our daughter's a genius." I step back when she's boring in like that. I wonder what kind of day care she's really running, let my imagination run wild, second-guess myself until my head's on fire with a migraine. But then I peek in the door and note again and again how happy all her charges are, how healthy and clean they look, how pleasantly occupied. All of them, of course, but one. *I'm being overprotective*, I tell myself. *I need to learn to let Jeremy out in the world. It's not me he needs, but time.*

⌒

AND THEN A good friend gets married in Atlanta, and for the first time since his birth, Jeremy and I will be apart. How disorienting it is to pack my bags and take a plane, put a book on my lap, start to read it. Once disembarked, I am surrounded by other friends of the bride's and sudden kaleidoscopic bits of conversation that make no sense to me because the sentiments seem so untroubled. Easy laughter, incidental stories, rumors, gossip, then the crowd pairing up and renting cars, rustling maps, forecasting grand adventures. Someone drives a spacious car. I sit in the back, watching the roadside advertisements above the yellow plains of Georgia, having nothing much to say.

It is a wedding of acronyms—M.D.'s, Ph.D.'s, D.M.D.'s—except me and the best man, who sells boilers in Caterpillar country. After vows, rings, kisses, cakes, I summon the nerve to track a pediatrician down and explain, in the quiet corner I drag him into, that I am worried about my son. "He hums these melodies," I say. "I can tell that he thinks these amazing thoughts. But he hardly looks at me and he rarely puts forth a sentence, and I don't know what to think. Am I being too sensitive?" The doctor studies me awhile, slumps against the brocaded wall of the reception room, and begins enumerating possibilities—perhaps there's something wrong with his ears? perhaps his development's delayed? perhaps he's not being engaged and he's bored?—debating with himself, it seems, instead of answering me. "I'd see a specialist," he says, at the end of all that, and then he's off, heeding an old friend who is waving from across the room.

What happens afterward is this: I escape to the city with two old friends and drive down three different roads named Peach to a faceless motel. We take a room on the motel's backside, where the neon from the Tattletale Inn next door doesn't shine. The talk is female, vaguely familiar, and I sink in, find myself in the center of one friend's story before I understand where it began. "It breaks my heart the way her whole life is seeping into his, but thank God they diagnosed it early," she's saying. "There's medication for cases like these, and lots of therapy, and in the best scenario, the child can be trained to break his own terror, can break some of the obsessions and patterns and merge, at least a little, with real life. But it's clear as day, the autism's

changed her whole life. Her husband wants to leave. She
has lost her family dreams."

Long after the room crawls to sleep, I lie awake listening
to the bang of doors and feet across the way. I imagine
Tattletale refugees—conjure up big men and broken-
toothed women striking glamorous poses from TV. I hear
the telltale money changing hands, or perhaps it is the
chink of ice. I can't tell. All that night, I think about that
mother struggling, and I grow frightened for her. I despair
over what my friend has said, how she has defined the word
autism. Preoccupation with inner thoughts, daydreams,
fantasies.

JEREMY DOES NOT remember me when I come home from
Atlanta. He stares past my eyes and runs in circles, and one
afternoon he flings himself, deliberately, from the top of
the interior stairs. I am right behind him, but not close
enough, and like the wooden Pinocchio, he falls and falls,
down the staircase. I stop taking him to the sitter. I stop taking Jeremy outside to see the boy next door. I start driving,
hours every day, so that he cannot run in circles, won't be
tempted to fly from the steps again; we were lucky enough
the first time. I am terrified, desperate. Despite the ghostly
silence that has stolen into my house, my head screams
with a noise that won't fade.

A few weeks later, Jeremy and I meet my mother at the
local shopping mall. It is a dark day, raining, the earth
molting beneath soggy leaves, and I have to admit that I
feel more than the usual degree of anxiety at the prospect
of this afternoon. I have been hiding something from my
mother, hiding Jeremy, and more than that, I am feeling
vulnerable, angry at my husband, who has begun to suggest

that something is wrong with Jeremy, that a doctor should be called. "Please be okay," I plead with Jeremy as I pull him from the car. "We'll be here for only an hour. Please be good."

But I can't lie my way out of trouble. My husband, my mother know that. I can't come in from the dismal rain with my hair all wet and my nerves all shot and my son in my arms, yet miles away. And I can't say things are good, and I can't say things are bad, and then blame it on myself when no one, maybe, is to blame. I can't say those things. I can't even speak. I can't believe how deep the hurt goes, or how black things look, how broken. "I know what's going on," my mother says, before the jackets are off, the stroller unpacked, before Jeremy, eyes averted, small hips bucking, finally submits to the stroller's seat belt. "I know a doctor. He's a friend of a friend. He's waiting for your call."

diagnosis

*W*e go on Halloween day, four o'clock in the afternoon. The sky is already falling, the air is pungent as split fruit, fires burn now in the evacuated bellies of pumpkins. The children next door, the children across the street, the children beyond the railroad tracks are devilish and impatient in their costumes: carefree. We hear their delighted screams, their practiced roars. We hear the admonitions of their parents. Instructions for the sane: *Don't scare your sister. Don't leave your little brother behind.* And now I pour the candy into a plastic orange drum and leave it beneath the porch light with a sign: *Take what is yours.* And now my husband separates Jeremy from the web of his play, one limb at a time, and Jeremy comes. Struggles and twists in his father's strong arms until he can see the glitter of matchbox cars no more. Until we are finally in the car and I have my dark glasses on and I am waving to the neighbors as if all were well. *Sorry, we'll miss you. Something came up. What poor timing this is, how terribly bothersome to have made these other plans.*

Maps on our laps, we drive. It is good to follow directions, to have some. It is all we discuss for an hour: the names of streets, the shapes of traffic; even Jeremy seems satisfied by the view. The sky bruises and heals, bruises. We are far from our own house on a concrete landscape, past the industrial parks, the airport, the refineries, past the tireless petroleum smells, and now the roads begin to narrow; we see trees again, houses. We have two more turns to take—a right, a left—and then everything changes. Two tall walls bracket the smooth yards of grass and the defoliated trees that come into view. A sign announces the hospital's name; yellow arrows on the asphalt light the way. The building appears beyond a grove of parked cars. It is a hunkered-down vessel of indeterminate hue that contains, we imagine, some kind of truth.

But everything is artifice. Everything, when we open the door, is not what it naturally is; there are distortions. A Queen of Hearts parades the lobby, her velvet staff prancing high in the air. A pregnant pumpkin rolls forward, lop-sided and ridiculous, in a paranormal orange rind. A cat expects kittens, an animation leaps to life, a receptionist says hello and takes our name while giant plastic ears flap at her head. "This is sick," I say to my husband, indignant, and he takes over at the desk, one health insurance card after another, while I hold Jeremy's hand, take him into a corner of the room and say, "That banana isn't real; look at its shoes. That zebra walking upright is a fake." It doesn't help much. Jeremy is overwhelmed, hides in my skirt. He doesn't see the humor in Halloween, and frankly, neither do I.

I look for comfort. I look backward and forward and think of the Celts, twenty-five centuries ago, who on this day burned the possessed in a Druid's bonfire, just because they had reached the denouement of their long summer. Just because it was assumed that last year's dead were coveting this year's living, looking for a heart, a pair of lungs, a bony cage of ribs within which to roost their disembodied souls. So the Celts, they dressed like goblins. The Celts, they dressed like witches, all disfigured, dressed like demons, horns on their heads, pitchforks mounted. They screamed bloody murder, and they doused the flames on their hearths, and in that manner they made their homes inhospitable to the pattering footsteps of evil. Then the Celts hollered their way to the edge of the town, where a fire raged beneath the care of an ancient Druid. Marched behind their masks looking for signs. They paraded, swooped, roared, and they studied the faces and gestures of those they traveled with, until they'd found the one or two who'd been possessed. Didn't matter who. Just mattered that when they found it, when on All Hallows' Eve some poor costumed soul displayed the suspect appearance of a dead man's habits, the common Celts, in the middle of that night, stomped it. Chased it through the streets and tossed it, a living person, into the height of the flames. Burned from the outside, it melted one layer at a time—costume, cottons, flesh, blood, ribs. The voice of its terror was the last thing to go. This was Halloween. This was the last day of summer. An object lesson to any other roving spirits contemplating possession of a human soul.

Today it is fruit. Today it is the rubber likenesses of politicians, and a pair of edible fangs, and a box of striped detergent walking sideways through a glass door. There are no bonfires. There are no Druid priests, and the nurses, the technicians, the administrators in this brick fortress are in good cheer, masquerading, for this moment, as something else, someone possessed—a candy cane, a cosmonaut— while my husband stands at the front desk talking insurance and I stand in the farthest corner of the room, my son's hand in my hand, my heart in my throat, my mind already fashioning excuses, defenses, working its way into the stories I must be careful not to tell. My son is innocent. My son is pure. Look at him. Look! He's not possessed.

—

WE ARE TAKEN to rooms, and we are tested. All three of us tested, because Jeremy isn't talking, and he isn't about to answer the questions posed first by the speech pathologist and then by the director of developmental medicine himself, the friend of my mother's friend. We are asked for our histories, and I take the lead: Jeremy was an exquisite baby, Jeremy is a blessing, sure there are differences, but they have a beauty, like the wrong-colored threads in a weave. "Slight deviations," I say. "Hell," I say, "he's the offspring of artists. I'm sure you've seen this mix before." I force a smile toward the doctor; she remains noncommittal. I look at Jeremy, lying with the doctor's cars on the carpet by our feet, bothering no one, impervious, or so it seems, to the dialogue overhead. I look at my husband and it's clear that my answers are not the answers he would give, if only I'd give him the chance to speak, if only I could stop leaning insistently forward in my plastic orange chair, trying to coax a clean bill of health from this doctor. I've left my coat on. I pull it around me. I lean back against the plastic and let my husband take the lead.

"Jeremy is very smart," my husband begins. "We know he is. He has an extraordinary memory, and you should see the impressive patterns that he makes, the geometry he can fashion with cars."

"Cars?" The doctor straightens the clipboard on her lap and pays attention.

"Matchbox cars. He arranges them in spirals. Or pin-

wheels. And the colors are right." My husband touches
Jeremy on the head as he says this, as if to let Jeremy
know that it is just fine to listen.

"The colors are right?" The doctor asks a clarifying question before she writes any of my husband's statement down.
Beneath us, Jeremy goes from his knees to his side and curls
his whole body around a yellow school bus.

"Aesthetic. Well considered."

"Hmm." The doctor writes. She looks at us. Cranes her
neck and looks at Jeremy.

"The intelligence is evident in more than the patterns,"
my husband continues. "For example. Jeremy was talking
very young. Labeling things before he turned one. Putting
a name to the pictures in books."

"Uh-huh." The doctor thumbs through the pages on her
clipboard to get to the right part of the form. "Tell me
more."

"Jeremy labeled the pictures," my husband says it again,
with greater confidence. "Pictures of boats. Pictures of
planes. Articles of clothing. Colors. He understood whatever he was looking at, and he would give it names."

"We'll test that," the doctor says. "We have vocabulary
exercises."

"He might not do everything here," I say, tilting forward
conspiratorially, wanting to win her favor. "He's much
more comfortable at home."

"We'll just have to see," the doctor replies. "Won't we?"

She wants to dismiss me and return to my husband, but
I won't let this go. "Think about it," I tell her. "This is a
brand-new place. Even the best of us struggle in an alien
landscape." My husband places his hand on my knee. It's a
sign between us; he continues.

"Jeremy is kind," he says, a new topic. "He's a bighearted kid. It's hard to explain, but we sense something about him that is larger than life. We know it's true."

"Larger than life." The doctor writes. She sits back. Folds her hands over her clipboard and studies all three of us, one at a time. I notice that she wears a wedding ring. I wonder if her children are at home, in their costumes, waiting for her. "Why are you here?" she asks us finally. "What concerns do you have for your son?"

"Jeremy is our only child," my husband says, after it is quiet for too long and I do not trust myself to speak. "We have nothing against which to compare his development."

"You want to know where he stands," the doctor says, rephrasing the question. "You want an assessment."

"We want to know he's *all right*," I say resentfully. "Or," and now I whisper, "*if* he is." I am desperate for this doctor's approval. I want her to say the right words. *You are excused.* I look at my husband. He is formulating his own list of responses and he is staring straight ahead.

"We're here because Jeremy might need some extra help," he says, at last. "We'd like your thoughts. Some ideas. Guidance. Simple games we could play to more completely engage him. In life. Us. Others. We're looking for recommendations. Exercises and activities that will unlock the good stuff he keeps inside." My husband turns and floods me with his Salvadoran eyes. I know those eyes: *Tell her the truth.* I slouch back into my coat again, and the examination, in earnest, begins.

━

IT WAS THE Romans, A.D. 61, who took the murder out of Halloween, replacing the sacrifice of neighbors with Egyptian-style effigies. It was the Irish, fleeing famine, who brought the revelry to the States, and it was a bit of lore involving a drunkard named Jack that launched the tradition of lanterned pumpkins. Trick-or-treating is European and is derived from All Souls' Day, though today chocolate, not soul cakes, is the currency of exchange, and the prayers are gone, they've vanished, as we beg from door to door.

It's getting later. Dark outside now, maybe even haunted, and the staffers who walk these corridors at this hour have exceeded the limit on their costumes. The spotted cow's udder droops depleted from her belly. The red clown wig has gone askew. The baby doll with her giant plastic bottle seems wizened and old, a little cranky. The nurses, the receptionists, the lab technicians, one social worker have done their thing, and now it is time for them to go home and leave this brand of medicine behind.

While patients straggle. Other parents walk the hallways with their children between them, a few thrown down wearily in the hard blue chairs that are bolted, one after another, to the cinder-block walls outside the interior examining rooms. Like us, they are waiting for the last appointments of the day, and when we choose to look up, we recognize their expressions. We apprehend a community of other broken hearts, families like ours who have forgone Halloween for the vaguest possibility of an answer. We pass by. We pace up and down, our coats and our son draped across our shoulders as we obey the unspoken rule: Thou shalt not trespass.

THE DIRECTOR OF developmental medicine is a generous man. At the end of this day, he makes room for our grieving, makes it possible for us to say what we really mean, to falter, to admit we are afraid. He reads the handwritten reports of the examiner who has gone before him and takes a long, thoughtful look at our son. He gives Jeremy a book to read, and Jeremy without coaxing pronounces, "Chick!"—an accurate summing-up of the picture on the torn book's cover. At this, my husband and I break into irresponsible elation, and the doctor gives us a moment to be proud, to reach out for Jeremy and hug him and say, "You are amazing, little boy. You really are so smart." Kindness, and this removes the barriers between us and what we have to hear, what we have yet to go through, more tests, more watching our son perform through the spectacles of science.

Or is it science? This is a small room. It is a white room, a rectangle. Whatever is elaborate or complex cannot be seen, not by me, I suspect not by my husband. The tools here, the technologies, are words and pictures, questions and answers, a rubber ball, a slim flashlight. It could not be more basic, more mysterious; it is impossible to locate, with any layman-like precision, the sorts of symptoms being measured. Impossible for us—my husband, me—to distinguish, by virtue of these tests, between that which is simply personality, mood, artistry, mutable, and that which is biology, chemistry, genetics, fixed. Give a boy a picture and ask, *What do you see?* and maybe, just maybe, his answer, *Dog,* is a joke on *Horse,* or maybe in his mind he has named the horse *Dog,* or maybe you have obstructed his eyesight with too much testing, or maybe, it's surely possible, the child wants to go home. Toss the child a ball, and when it doesn't land in his hands, maybe you report, *Well, look at that. Baseball is not his sport.* Throw a pale string of light across the tattered carpet and ask the boy to walk a straight line, and maybe, when he doesn't, he is speaking to you, saying as loud as he knows how, *I am a person, not some experiment.*

But the doctor, after a long spell of tests like these—questions, musings, simple gazings toward our child's huge averted eyes—draws his preliminary conclusions, and because he is kind, because he is patient, because he has made room for our hearts at this hour of Halloween, we bend in close and listen, freezing the words in our minds to extract their meaning. "This first round of testing supports an understanding of autistic features, but not strict autism," he begins. "We see atypical language development, echolalia, that tendency to repeat just what he's heard. We see an absence of semantic associations; I'm particularly concerned with his pragmatics—his ability to use language and gestures in social situations to acquire what he may need. Reciprocal interaction is a challenge for your son; we see him struggling with this, we hear your frustration, we understand that he's not picking up on the everyday cues. Fine and gross motor skills are underage. And yes, Jeremy does exhibit behavioral oddities—perseveration, narrow interests, difficulty in shifting from task to task, a tendency toward withdrawal; at times your son shuts down. But this is preliminary. We'd like to see your son again, give him a few more tests so as to understand things better."

My husband breathes. I don't. Jeremy, impatient, has started running in his circles at our feet. Then he starts to cry. He's had it with testing and he wants to get home; I reach into my bag and retrieve some Cheerios, then pull him onto my lap and hope he'll eat.

"You'll want a lot of help for Jeremy," the doctor goes on. "But let's not think too far ahead, just yet. Let's do a few more tests and let's meet again near Christmas. See how things go. In the meantime, you'll want stricter rules in your house and a consistent pattern of rewards. You could use food, you could use words to encourage better eye contact, more pragmatics, fewer incidents of withdrawal. Let Jeremy know what you're looking for. Be adamant and clear; don't bend. Don't parent individually. Cases like this, especially, take a team. And when he gets locked in, when you get locked out, remove him, right away, from his environment. Pick him up. Change his perspective. Don't let him lie on that carpet anymore with his cars. He needs new stimuli, a constant stream of them. He needs release from his obsessions. Don't let him go on for more than twenty minutes at the same activity."

"What about the future?" I start to ask, and the doctor says, "I have no crystal ball. Your son is two and a half years old; so much can change, in one direction or another. I can only make forecasts, and at this point, in the absence of the additional tests, I'd say that he'll find one thing he's good at and make of that thing his career. He could succeed, for example, in a job that requires little social chitchat. Computers are a possibility. Artistry. But he's going to have it rough, you need to know that. You need to know that he reads the world a different way, that words have little context for him, moods are immaterial. He'll need help deciphering social cues, but all of us, eventually, have to make it on our own. He'll have to work harder than the rest of us. He'll have to accept whatever's missing. You'll have to accept those things as well, and you'll have to do it without assigning blame. No one is at fault here. Not Jeremy, for his genetics, and not you, for bringing him into the world. Let's keep our sights on December. Let's see where we are at that point."

⌐

THE SKY SEEMS spooked as we leave the hospital. The naked finger of a towering tree pokes a hole through the moon, and the smattering of stars sheds little light. The car is easy to find, nevertheless—virtually alone on this abandoned parking lot—and without saying a word, I help myself into the car's backseat, so as to sit beside my son, to study him beneath the wholly inadequate lamp of this night. He is exhausted, and he lets me hold his hand, and I am grateful for the silence, for the radio that my husband does not tune in to, from where he sits, far away, in this car.

We drive. Jeremy turns his head toward his window, and after a while I turn my eyes toward mine. The companion cars on this highway are manned by grotesque and malformed drivers, ordinary people masked to the nines just for fun. "Get serious," I say. "Jesus. Don't these people have something grown-up to do?"

"It's Halloween," my husband cautions. "Give them a break. Tomorrow they'll wake up, and all they'll be is who they are."

We haven't eaten. It's way past dinnertime and we can't imagine a restaurant we want to go to, someplace on earth that won't offend us with its shrill customers. By now my husband has lost the directions, and he's driving for nothing, going where the roads go, and both of us know it doesn't matter. We have no one waiting on us and nowhere to hide, no fantasy to slip into or out of, no roving spirits that we have the power to slay, no prayer that enters our hearts, and tomorrow, when we wake up, nothing will be any different than it is now, at this haunted hour. And the next day, and the next day, maybe things will never change. Or maybe Jeremy will engage, emerge, evolve, and maybe I will learn how to build a household of rules, learn how to mother firmly, learn how to interfere with the precious patterns of my son's endangered world, learn, even, how to trust his growth to someone else, to therapy—where will

we find it? how? No one, not even science, can edge us closer, help us see. Words, approximations, muddy crystal balls
are all there is. Words are it for us right now. Everything
else is the same.

"I bet the mall is open," I say, after nothing has been said
for a while.

"Does it ever close?" my husband complains quietly. "Do
shoppers tire?"

"It's Halloween," I tell him. "Halloween. You know." I
touch my face. It's soaking wet. I try to breathe. There is no
air.

"I know what's what," he says. "I can see." His voice is
distant, his hands on the wheel.

"We never bothered to get Jeremy a costume, and now
look at this," I say, "it's Halloween." I brush the water from
beneath each eye, but the rain on my dark face remains.

"There'll be other years," my husband consoles me.

"I suppose so."

"Other Halloweens."

"But this one's gone," I say, as if it were important. "And
we never even got him a costume."

"Some parents."

"Some. Christ, I hope he forgives us." I turn to look at
Jeremy. He is fast asleep at last, his fingers loosely curled
inside my hand.

"What do you think he'd want to be," my husband asks
me, finally, "if he could tell us?"

"A hat?" I ask.

"A car?"

"Patterns," I say. "His own design. God. He'd be brilliant, wouldn't he?" I lean my head back against the fabric
of the car, close my eyes, imagine my son in a costume.
Imagine him giggling and ridiculous, demanding atten-

tion, impatiently awaiting Halloween. I am suddenly worn out, weary. I want to rest now, too, dream, like Jeremy dreams. "Do you know where we are yet?" I ask my husband. "Shouldn't we almost be home?"

"We're getting there," he answers me.

aftermath

I want to believe in the misdiagnosed, but see: he is not altogether well. He escapes to a room in his head like a ship to sea, even as the gulls fly above, imploring: land, land.

I am earth beneath storm, the air inside a snapped reed. I scream my helpless anger into an empty room.

looking for help

*B*etween Halloween and Christmas we make two more trips to the children's hospital to give Jeremy more time with the specialists. At home I exercise one of the few pieces of first-consultation advice that I can actually translate into daily living: do not, under any circumstance, let him get stuck. Do not let him lie on the floor or on the street the way he wants to, nose pressed against his perfect parade of toy cars. Don't let him sit in his high chair dropping his juice cup on the floor so that I can pick it up and he can drop it and I can pick it up and he can drop it. Don't let him pace back and forth as we know he wants to, don't let him rock, don't let his mind race so fast no one can catch it. Don't let anything go on for more than twenty minutes; forcibly remove him from the scene. Pick him up—screaming and kicking, hollering, raging with all of his might— and drag him from one zone to another. Be vigilant. Guard against lockouts. He is still very young; his brain is forming.

It seems to me that I have but two options: the stroller and the car. Jeremy knows what he wants and he's a willful child, and he's extremely intelligent besides. He is not going to accept me idling up with a new distraction, then attend to it with mild surprise. He's not going to be dislodged easily; he has his passions, just like I do, and no clever sleight of hand is going to make him a traitor to his own mind. And so what becomes of us is that I begin with five firm warnings and then, at the twenty-minute mark, I physically extract him from his play. In good weather, my destination is typically the stroller, into which I strap him—bucking and wrathful, sobbing, insulted—before taking off at a mad dash down the street. Out of sight of the immediate neighborhood, where Jeremy can collect himself in peace. We walk for hours—hours—up the hills, circling playgrounds, the library, the autumn trees with their molten leaves, me leaning over Jeremy when he is quieter, calm, when I can beg him to forgive me. *Please, Jeremy. Please. This is for your own good. Maybe someday you'll believe me.*

With the approach of winter and the shortening of the days, I begin relying increasingly on the car. It's a better option for Jeremy but a difficult one for me, as I—now working a steady midnight shift for the magazines—am ragged with lack of sleep and worried about my performance behind the wheel. I drive only down the local streets, attempt no highways, no passing lanes or blind-spotted mergers, and sometimes, in the nauseous haze of a relentless migraine, I pull into a superstore parking lot, turn off the ignition, and throw my head against the seat. Jeremy's patience with such tactics doesn't last long. I make it up to him by pretending that we have business at the store— unstrap him, carry him inside, walk dazed and off-balance up and down the aisles until we find the selection of matchbox cars. I know that I'm bolstering the very thing I'm responsible for inoculating against, but I sit there with him on the grungy floor of the superstore, taking every last car off the rack. Trying to admire them the way that he does, imagine them in a long, sinewy line. We always leave the store with at least one matchbox purchase. I'm short the fortitude required to deny him.

The darker the days get, the more we seem to buy. Soon I'm spending forty dollars a day on things we don't need with money we definitely don't have, and I'm starting to wonder if it's me who's compulsive and antisocial, and Jeremy the understanding, healthy one. No matter how dumb this is, how small-minded and uncreative, how alien to a woman with a history of drawing up activity lists, I cannot seem to break the pattern, can think of only one thing to do at ten in the morning when a twenty-minute shutdown sets in: get in the car and drive, park in the lot and shop, take my little boy to his favorite department and buy him anything that he seems to say he wants. I am looking for distractions during a difficult time. I am doing my best, and it is pitiful.

A FEW DAYS before Christmas, we have another consult at the hospital, a final summing-up with the original doctor. The specialists who have seen Jeremy have typed up their opinions, and my parents, two of Jeremy's greatest fans, have joined us for the session. A nurse has taken Jeremy to another room, where he is playing, we are told, and very peaceful.

The doctor begins by telling us that Jeremy's markedly improved since Halloween: he's making daring attempts at eye contact, expresses endearing curiosity, and has many of his own words back, though he is 75 percent echolalic. This spurt of development has thrown off the evaluation a bit, but the specialists have separately rendered their opinions: pervasive developmental disorder not otherwise specified

(PDDNOS) from the psychologist; moderate pragmatic disorder with atypical features from the speech/language pathologist. The primary physician has his opinion, too: the label he would prefer to use is developmental language disorder with atypical features. Specifically, reading directly from the report, he says: "We said that although he has a number of atypical features such as his echolalia and his getting withdrawn and getting locked into an activity, his intelligence, as best as we can measure it in such a small child, is well within the normal range. We also said that it is very unlikely that this is an overestimate of his true cognitive abilities, but it may, indeed, be an underestimate. . . . His individual receptive and expressive language skills were also in the normal range. This is in spite of his difficulty with the pragmatics of language. We said that some of the features that he shows are, indeed, those of an autistic child, but he does not have enough of them or any of them to a severe enough degree to warrant the diagnosis of autistic. In fact . . . he looks for interactions in a way that would not be characteristic of an autistic child."

All that said, the doctor continues, Jeremy will indeed need individual attention, small classrooms, a special course of therapy, though what that therapy is and where we are to get it is not in the pages of the report. The social worker has prepared a small packet, but when I spill its contents out on the table, I find a collection of pamphlets directed at the parents of autistics. Nutritional pointers. Disciplinary suggestions. Support groups for the grieving parent. What I want is the name of the person to call. Something—anything—but now we are heading home, the future a blank book with so many uncut pages. "What *was* that?" I ask my husband finally, after Jeremy's fallen asleep.

"What was what?" he asks, in a withdrawn voice. He is

driving. I'm in the back. I have thrown him out of a very private place, but I am feeling agitated, somewhere between angry and mournful, and I need his attention for a moment. I'm persistent.

"All those labels? Which one is the one? Which one fits?" I turn and look at Jeremy and his radiant beauty, try to side with one or the other of the decrees. All I see is his giftedness, his otherworldly qualities, how even in the fit of a dream he's reached for me, grabbed my finger with his hand. I see his black hair and his feathered eyelids and I am reminded about acts of mercy, how God sent him, this saintly creature, into the clutter of my home. As if I deserved anything nearly this gorgeous. As if I would know what to do when he arrived.

"Jeremy's different," my husband says, after a while. "They don't have any labels for what he is."

"No," I say quietly. "I guess that they don't."

"He's half you and he's half me," my husband continues. "That's all."

"Way out of the language zone," I concur, wearily. "Our little boy. Nothing describes him."

AND YET I do want words. I want the clarity and comfort I have all my life found in the company of books, but mornings spent reading in the antique rocker prove bewildering and emotionally costly. Failing to find *pervasive developmental disorder not otherwise specified* in the family medical dictionary, I turn to the entry marked *autism* and read, in part, *The outlook for autistic children is guarded. Some, particularly those who at one time appeared to be developing normally and then regressed, may eventually become marginally self-sufficient and independent. But most require life-*

long shelter and care. I close the book—hurt, dissatisfied, angry enough to keep looking. But I find no comfort, no comfort at all, when I finally locate the elusive label in a book. *PDD as defined in DSM III refers to disorders that in the past have been called childhood schizophrenia, childhood psychosis, symbiotic childhood psychosis, and other names.* Ancient history, I mutter. Voodoo medicine. Slamming that book shut, I read on and on, feel like I'm floating, an unharbored ship, until I'm back to autism and a set of apparent synonyms, a caution issued by a physician in another book. *Instead of hearing that their child has classic autism, parents are more likely to hear labels like "Pervasive Developmental Disorder," "Atypical Pervasive Developmental Disorder," "Autistic-like," or "Pervasive Developmental Disorder Not Otherwise Specified." It is important to remember that, regardless of their label, the education and treatment of these children is the same.*

I can hardly comprehend what I am reading, though one thing does grow infuriatingly clearer: *pervasive developmental disorder not otherwise specified* has the experts stymied all over the world. They can't even agree on the terminology. *The PDD concept is problematic for a number of reasons,* I read in a medical journal. *First, whereas autistic disorder is defined on a basis of seemingly stringent diagnostic criteria, PDD is more loosely defined. Second, the term PDD is inconsistent, in that it does not refer to all PDDs (e.g., mental retardation is not included) and the "pervasiveness" of the disorders included in the category is arguable: existing evidence suggests that the disorders are "specific" or "partial" rather than pervasive. Further, the empirical underpinnings of this class of disorders are less satisfactory than those of some overlapping concepts. There is, for example, much clearer support for Lorna Wings' . . . category: the triad of social, language, and behavioral impairments.*

Cause? Interventions? Prognosis? I grow impatient with the desire for at least one answer, but the debate rages on the pages that I'm now reading. Good news: over time, in the luckiest of cases, some autistic-like traits can be controlled. Bad news: this is a chronic disorder and there is no cure; development may be erratic, adolescence may bring deterioration, the child is in this for life. Good news: the experts no longer believe that the condition is caused by the inadequate love and caretaking of the parents. Bad news: the most anyone seems willing to say right now is that autism and related disorders are biologically determined; there *is* a genetic component. The clinicians are performing autopsies, MRI and PET scans, and neurophysiological exams. They're analyzing plasma and platelets and urine. They're checking on links between autism and tuberous sclerosis, Rett syndrome, and fragile X; studying prenatal and birth "insults" to the brain; investigating basic psychological deficits; experimenting with therapies ranging from massive doses of vitamin B_6 to intensive behavioral modification—but I've lost the capacity to follow the argument, I'm getting plowed under by terms no one ever said a parent would have to understand, and besides—and this is the most essential point—*I don't see Jeremy on any of these pages.* Not even close. It is true. One can make a list of his traits and say: he has obsessions, his speech and his gestures are not yet pragmatic, he isn't flexible, he wants very desperately to be alone. And a lot of this might look like whatever the experts want to call it, *but don't stop there.* Because my son's compelling. He's confoundingly bright. He's artistic. He's affectionate. He's gentle as a new bird in the cup of your hands, and none of this surfaces from the pages on my lap, none of these traits are celebrated by the clinicians, looked into, explored, explained. Anger is a salve, and I allow myself that anger, that rage, that release of divine umbrage, as in the rocker, in the dark, before the sun has cracked the sky, I pound the books, the Xeroxed pages with my fist. I pledge to the boy and to his father, both sleeping above me, that I will not, *no matter what,* confuse my child with a label. I will not be taken down by false constructions, empty forecasts. I will not lose sight of the gift that my son is, will not let go of my expectation—my surety—that Jeremy will find his way into this world.

⟶

NEWS GETS AROUND. My next-door neighbor asks the genuine question. My husband makes infinitesimal disclosures at work. My sister calls a friend because the friend might know something, and the wind carries the news back to us. Little signals. Little prayers. Someone says, *I know a therapist.* Another says, *There is a school.* Someone else remembers hearing about a failproof method on TV. Suddenly, acutely, we're on the other side of life.

The first therapist we go to is a woman, many towns away. We have gotten her name from the spouse of a colleague, and when I talk to her she sounds appropriate—experienced, unthreatening. I trust her place of business as soon as we pull in: a tall, brightly painted building with a spiraling stair, unconventionally apportioned rooms, wood floors, windowsills deep as a library shelf. There is something about elevators that has always seemed chilling—those dangerous pings, those cautionary red and green lights—and this building is too good for that, too turn-of-the-century sprawling.

The therapist herself seems pleasant and kind—a beau-

tiful woman with short red hair. She sets Jeremy up at a little white table and pulls a doll-sized chair beneath her,
leaving me with the room's only other chair, at a spectator's
distance. From shelves beside the table, she selects an arse-
nal of simple toys: plastic teddy bears no taller than a seg-
ment of my thumb, friendly creepy crawlers, scaled-down
windup toys such as the ones they give away with 99-cent
lunches. She gives Jeremy a handful of bears to hold—a
peace offering, an indication that the point here is to be
friends—and these slip through his fingers indifferently,
clattering onto the tabletop, a few leaping down to the floor.
Jeremy has his thumb in his mouth and his eyes rotated up
to the window. Without blinking, the therapist winds up a
mechanical toy, sets it running, cackling, whizzing on the
tabletop, over to Jeremy's side.

"Jeremy," I coach from my corner, "look at all those silly
toys. Aren't they funny, Jeremy? Take a look."

"I'll handle this," the therapist tells me, not turning her
head. "If his reactions aren't accurate right here at the
start, we won't have a level playing field," she explains.
"We need to determine our baselines."

"Sorry," I say, wrapping one leg around the other and
nesting my chin in my hand, diminishing myself. "I didn't
know the rules."

The windup rabbit has petered out on Jeremy's side of
the table; it is wheezing no more. "Send the bunny back to
me, Jeremy," the therapist urges, in her gentle, little-person
voice. "Do you know how to make it wiggle? Look." She
takes an extra one from the shelf. "Turn this little white
knob," she demonstrates, "and you can make the bunny
hop."

Jeremy shifts his gaze and stares at this red-haired

woman, as if he were seeing her for the first time that day and can't quite determine her purpose. Confused, he throws a quick glance across her shoulder, stands, and runs at a diagonal through the room, toward me. Instinctively, I put my arms out and smile. "You're doing a good job," I tell him, when only he can hear. I kiss him on the nose and stroke his hair.

"Don't encourage him," she warns. I know she's used her nicest voice, but I'm easily offended. She turns to face me now. "Maybe it would be better if you waited for us outside." There's nothing mean about her, but I'm insulted.

He's my son, I almost flash back, though I manage, at the very last moment, to exchange the sentiment with a more civilized, "He's getting acclimated. This is all new. I think my leaving would be disruptive."

"We'll see how it goes," she offers. "I've been doing this sort of therapy for a long time, and sometimes I've seen the parents help and sometimes I've seen just the opposite." She calls Jeremy back to the table, and obediently I lead him there, kiss him briefly, walk backward to my own miserable corner, and wait. There are fifteen minutes left in the half-hour appointment, and outside the walls of this room, I hear the noises of a nearby playground—children bundled up against the cold, swinging higher and higher, scraping the tepid sun with the soles of their shoes.

───

ONCE A WEEK, for the next several weeks, we make our way to the therapist. She keeps notebooks about the progress we're making, and because I am behaving, I am allowed to stay in the room, given five minutes at the end of each session to share observations of my own, the previous week of Jeremy's history. With her buckets of toys, the therapist gradually elicits Jeremy's attention, and sometimes he does the exercises right, and sometimes he allows himself to speak, halting, confidence-lacking phrases that mostly mimic whatever the therapist has said.

"Put the bear in the cup," she'll tell him.

"Put the bear in the cup."

"Now put the bear aahnn the cup."

"Bear aahnn the cup."

"Good, Jeremy."

"Good, Jeremy."

"Okay."

"Okay."

At first I am delighted by the sound of my son's voice, more voice than he has yielded now for months, but then the echoing becomes increasingly disturbing, becomes all there is in his speech, and I ask her, "What can we do about that?" though I know full well that the doctor, in all kindness, had prescribed food. Treats when he doesn't echo. No treats when he does.

"Jeremy's echolalia is particularly severe," she answers. "We don't see that degree of severity eradicating itself—"

"Overnight," I finish her sentence.

"No. We don't see it eradicating. Period. Lessening, yes. But we haven't seen a case like his that finally vanished without a trace."

"What are you saying?" I ask her. It is the last five minutes of the session, and with Jeremy now rocking impatiently on my lap, I discreetly cover his ears so he won't hear.

"You're going to have to accept some things," she tells me quietly, speaking over his head. "Remember where we

are, and where we've come from. His social interactions are
on the way up. He is becoming more engaged with the
world. Echolalia as a problem is persistent, but we're doing
the best that we can."

"What are you saying?" I ask her, an echo of myself.

"I think that now that we are seeing progress, you should
be doing more for your son," she replies, calmly. "Providing
him with more opportunities for interacting with children
his age. We can do that here. There's another child I'm
working with. I'd like to see the two together. Get them to
play games. Take cues from one another."

"Not yet," I say. "Please. Let's continue to fight this
echolalia."

VERY LITTLE ADDITIONAL ammunition is required. With
the uncanny sense of timing that Jeremy indubitably has,
he wakes up one morning within a week of that conversation and says, before I do, "Juice."

"You want juice?" I ask him. "Orange juice?"

He doesn't repeat what I said. He nods.

"Well then," I say. "Well then, you surely must have it."
I rustle up the tallest glass in the house and shake the carton exuberantly before pouring. I pick him up and lower
him into his high chair, then I sit catercornered from him,
just staring. I don't want to give him a sentence he can
repeat. I don't want to break this fragile moment.

He relishes his morning drink. A froth has collected on
his lip, a pulpy mustache. We don't talk much more and the
house begins to feel too quiet, so I release him from his
high chair, carry him upstairs, plop him on the couch. I go
to the cabinet and choose a record we can dance to, then I

sweep him back into my arms. He doesn't resist my power-
ful embraces. He seems happy to be dancing, his smile
tipped up and over, into his eyes.

The music is, perhaps, too loud. Someone else would
probably find it offensive. I want to keep dancing like this,
with the wall of sound up all around us, but I remember
Jeremy's delicate eardrums and do the parental thing.
When I stoop to turn the volume down low, he says, "You're
friends with the teacher."

Instead of lowering the music, I turn the whole sound
off, stand Jeremy on the floor beside me, and kneel to catch
his eyes. "What did you say?" I ask slowly.

"You're friends with the teacher," he repeats.

"The teacher is *your* friend, Jeremy," I say slowly. "She's
helping you learn lots of new things."

"Your friend," he says, nodding.

I don't pursue the fine pronomial distinction. It seems
like the smallest of problems. "Hey, thanks for telling me
about your friend," I tell him. "Finding out what you're
thinking makes me feel very special." I take Jeremy in my
arms again and hug him silly. I'm beside myself. We've
gone an hour without an echo, and he has told me something personal. It's almost like having a conversation.

Jeremy doesn't echo anything I say that day. He does get
stuck with his cars—grows infuriated when the slope of the
floor interferes with the car patterns he's making, acts dis-
gusted with me when I ineptly try to help. He won't look at
me when I finally separate him from the floor, screams to
high heaven because he has not, in his mind, finished the
job, and we're out strolling much of the day, I'm pointing
out birds and trees and neighbors, telling him stories,
singing him songs, trying to win him back; eventually

Jeremy calms down. All day I wait to hear myself thrown back on the wind, but it turns out that the echo is gone. "You want juice," he announces, after he decides to speak to me again. "You don't want your hat." Again I think: *Pronominal reversals are a minor inconvenience.* I call my husband at work. I call my mother. I yell to my neighbor, when she appears on her stoop. I don't have the maturity not to crow, but Jeremy's mien suggests he's done nothing very special. He's almost embarrassed about my exuberant reaction, so I bottle it, best as I can.

The next week at therapy I tell his new "friend" the story, tell her how the echo's been gone, the past few days. "There's that complication with the pronouns," I mention cavalierly, "but it looks like he's beat the odds with the echolalia."

Jeremy gets a therapeutic squeeze and a chance to prove himself. The therapist experiences the miracle for herself: the echo is gone. The focus of the next several minutes becomes the pronominal reversals, which seem exaggerated, in the absence of the echoes. At the close of the session, the therapist reiterates her belief that it's time to bring in the other little boy, and though I have my reservations about pressing the social issue too soon, I don't express them. I have to acknowledge that she has made a difference with echoes, and perhaps she can make things happen in the area of social play as well.

BUT THE PLAY sessions don't go well from the first, and they never do get better. Jeremy shuts down as soon as the other child makes his appearance, and there's nothing the therapist can do to tease him back out of his shell. Jeremy doesn't like having to share the bears with this child, or the table, or the therapist; he finds the whole thing absurd and agitating—and now I have to sit outside in the hallway, and this is the biggest effrontery of all. The therapist is honest about the extent of the problem, though I require few details. At home, the volume of anxiety rises dramatically, his exclusive interest in cars notches to a higher level, and he's more skittish than ever in the company of anyone outside his immediate home. My husband and I kid each other halfheartedly about what we would do if we could go on a date. But it's not in the cards.

It seems that I'm either driving or walking the whole day long, perpetually interfering with Jeremy's passions. Or sometimes, lonely, with an achiness of heart, I give up and lie on the floor beside him and watch the cars rolling nowhere in sequence. It's quiet then, and Jeremy's peaceful. Suddenly I'm not the oafish thing that interrupts him. I'm a spectator in the prismatic world that he adores mastering, creating.

We try the social sessions for a number of weeks; finally we all agree that they're premature. We make one last trip to the therapist's office for a consultation, where we review progress, get a few tips about the nettlesome pronomial reversals, and lay out plans for the months ahead. The therapist suggests a speech-enriched camp—small class size, great instructors, the right thing for Jeremy many weeks from now, when surely he'll be over his fears. She also suggests an enriched toddler gym program, where Jeremy can begin to hone his fine and gross motor skills.

"Does Jeremy like to color?" the therapist asks.

"Not yet." Strange to think that she's never asked that question before.

"Is he riding a bike? A pair of Big Wheels?"

"Not yet. But then he doesn't have much of a chance, does he? I'm either pushing him or driving him all day long."

"I think these are issues. You should have them addressed."

"Nobody dances the way Jeremy does," I tell her. "Besides, I'm athletic and so is my husband; surely he inherited those genes."

"Don't let it go too long," she encourages kindly. "You have to treat the whole disorder."

WHAT ARE YOU treating, what are you looking for, in the programs you begin to assess? What aspect of the disability are you to write off as incurable, and what are you to fight for? What combination of person and place will yield the highest results? No time to lose, no second chances, and I am calling the toddler gym programs now, interviewing the directors, listening for a kindness in the telephone voice, for an interregnum where I can stop and reveal, *But my child will be different from the rest, is that okay?* Calling the nursery schools in my part of town, saying, *Is your program enriched? Can you make an exception? Will you meet him at least? He's incredible.* And when the voice on the line says too quickly, *Sign him up,* I conclude that the program will be lacking. And when the voice discriminatingly reports, *Our program isn't right for your son,* I am convinced that it is the best place around. I hang up, enraged. I hang up, cursing intolerants and bigots, the conceit of the everyday world. There's an irony at work here, but I'm not willing to admit it.

It goes in circles, and finally I make a selection, dress my son in a red sweat suit, and drive to the most humane gym.

Where there are blue mats and a charming tunnel and Lego-colored climbers in strategic locales on the floor. A craft table with a spill of pinecones and glitter, and a tall man in a goofy clown suit that makes me wonder, right off the bat, *Is this for real?* The kids are happy and the mothers are chatting, but I don't trust myself to join the clusters of grown-up talk. There's the secret I am harboring, after all, and there's the thing I've just remembered: it's been months since I've taken a stroll through real life, and I'm not sure I have the skills for the occasion.

Jeremy is on his own. He's running the big, warehouse-shaped room in clockwise fashion, hurdling obstacles—a throwing ball, a bouncing ball, a little girl in diapers—with the grace he was born with. I slouch against the gypsum wall and let him go, telling myself that his antics are a natural reaction; he's adjusting. The clown says hello in a baritone voice, and I give him the check that I've promised. "We'll start with the parachute in five minutes or so," he tells me. "This part, right now, is just warm-up."

Happy toddler music is playing in the background, and Jeremy, flush in the face, is rounding the corner on another lap. "Hey, Rascal," I call for him. "Check this out. Look at the pinecones you'll be painting."

He keeps running. Hurdles a plastic baseball bat, swings wide around the slide set, inadvertently kicks the ball that another little kid has been chasing.

"Parachute time," the clown man calls, and the *whee* of joy ricochets through the room as all the little gymnasts disembark their climbers, tunnels, mothers' sides, and go skittering to the center of the room. Jeremy is new to this and does not know the routine, so I track him down, catch him in my arms, and carry him to the rayon circle on the floor. Put him in front of me, pinch a piece of fabric into his hands, and hold him with my knees, my arms, so that he cannot carry out another plan.

The clown starts parceling out rhythms and directions, and the fabric circle goes up above our heads, snapping and falling on the artificial breeze, while the little ones below zealously praise it. Passionate praises. Screams of delight, their mothers smiling. Maybe I've been home too long, but even I am touched by the parachute's magic. "Look at it fly," I tell Jeremy. "Look at the colors." But I have let down my defenses in the split of that second, and Jeremy has suddenly vanished. Out to the edge of the room again, running his laps, leaving me with a tenuous grip on the fabric.

⟶

WE FALL INTO a pattern. I take him to gym class and he runs a vigorous circle while I stand on the perimeter, feeling desperate but uncertain how to stop him. On the first day of the six-week summer camp program, I take him there and, against my better judgment, leave him in the arms of the teacher before he's calm. Turn my back on him. Trust his adjustment to this brand-new environment to someone other than me. *Separation anxiety is best managed firmly, with clean breaks*, the expert I'd consulted had told me. *Don't let Jeremy think he can persuade you to stay with his crying.*

The other children in Jeremy's group present a variety of disorders—everything from extreme timidity to a nearly undetectable slur in speech to a brain disorder I've never seen before and don't know how to handle. I get to know these children, one by one, for within the first day, within the first hour, in fact, the teacher calls and in an unnerved voice asks me to please, as quickly as possible, return to the school. "I can't calm him down," she says over the phone.

"We're not having this problem with the others." This is precisely what I had most feared would happen, and I'm furious with myself for having followed the advice of an expert. I will never, I tell myself, be misinformed by an "expert" again, and now I'm back in the car, running up the school steps, opening the door to the classroom, finding Jeremy in the teacher's arms. Relieved beyond words to see me, he buries his head in my skirt and wraps his arms fiercely around me. It takes several moments before I can lift him up into my arms. "I'm sorry," I tell him. "I'm sorry. I shouldn't have left you like that." He seems to forgive me, but it will take weeks to regain his trust—several weeks before he takes his eyes off me, turns his back, exhibits confidence that I won't leave him. I'm at his side every step of the way during the six-week summer session.

As the only mother in attendance, I must learn to learn my place. It's trial by error. As Jeremy's mother, I recognize that my first responsibility is to keep my son calm—able to focus, willing to move about the room and take things in. As an adult among young ones, I am also entrusted with minor classroom mishaps and general well-drawn rules—I mop up spilled paint, help the blonde into fresh clothes, supervise hand-holding and red lights during field trips to the firehouse, pour the pink juice into Dixie cups just after recess.

But as a woman lacking the qualifications of a certified professional, I must be careful to express no opinion on classroom structure, dynamics, or content. I retreat to the back of rooms, clear every impulse with a teacher, never question or instigate. When the children bicker among themselves, I ask what words to use before intervening. When a child screams unhappily at the project set before him, I know not to interpose. When a child climbs too high on a bright play structure, I ask the therapist, *Is his fear all right? Is it acceptable? Am I allowed to comfort him?* And when a child takes a positive step toward her apparent destination, I understand that it's the teacher's right to praise, something she's earned, though at times I sneak a quick high five onto the child's palm or kiss her on the cheek when no one's looking. I feel reduced and inadequate, and that feeling is compounded when some of the other mothers associated with this school seem to assume that I'm just an extra set of hands. *Could you get so-and-so's coat?* they've called out to me during pickup time. *I'm on the car phone; could you get him? Did you make sure you washed so-and-so's hands? Why are so-and-so's shoes so dirty today? Did she forget to wear her smock?* I'm the only mother who's been asked to stay, as I've said, and this is how I learn my place.

At the end of the day, I drive home full of questions. I wonder if the program's right for Jeremy, wonder if we're making progress, wonder what progress looks like, after all. There are no hard-and-fast rules. No one's offered any markers. No one has said, *Here's a development chart. Here are the milestones. Here are the intervals. Here's how far along you need to be. Here's how far you'll go.* I don't know if we're falling behind or doing the best we can do. I don't know what else is out there, what the finite universe of possibilities contains. I don't know whether I'm being over-anxious or undervigilant, terribly aggressive or irrefutably passive. Frustrated and at the end of my rope, I'm back on the phone making calls. Follow tips, rumors, advertisements in scattershot fashion as I try to plan for the fall, tap into the right play group, redress the mysterious imbalance of things. I call a school for the autistic; it sounds too extreme. I look for socialization programs; I'm not successful. I call, quite simply, a girl from the church, a woman from the local college, a teenager down the street and ask if they can spell me for a good price, help out with the stroller, provide my son with another point of view, new ideas about play, little distractions. Looking for environments, looking for cures, looking for an answer on the end of the line, I have begun, I suddenly realize, revealing secrets to perfect strangers: "My son needs a friend."

But friends, as it turns out, are in awfully short supply these days, and nobody is sparing any extras.

one sudden, quiet knowing

I have stopped sleeping. I have stopped closing my eyes at night, and sometimes I don't even go to bed, just stay downstairs, in a small room, and write. In front of the computer, I drift in and out, can't remember what I'm supposed to be doing, where I am going. More and more, I find myself thinking of Robin, though I knew her only vaguely and am not likely to encounter her again.

We met just twice. The first time: July 4; the backyard of an architect friend. Maybe she was twenty-eight, maybe I was twenty-four, but no one failed to notice that Robin was the woman and I the girl. She had a pornographic figure, so cute and spunky I thought at once of the Barbie doll. Her shorts were azure-colored, brief, easily lifted by the tongue of warmed air. Her shirt was a modest Izod, her feet bare, her blond hair feminine and effortless about her neck.

In the stilled-life freeze-frame I carry of Robin, she is laughing—sun on her teeth, hand in her husband's, eyes out beyond the suburban deck where her girls, aged five and three, are skipping, stark naked, between the meager fingers of a lawn sprinkler. She's laughing, but at the same time she's saying, ironic humor in her voice, "Just look at

that. Two little girls and already they love being naked."
Maybe Robin wasn't all doll when she laughed, but the
impression she made had its impact.

I sit somewhere behind Robin on the deck in that freeze-
frame, catching the sun but not casting a shadow. I sit in a
loose dress that hides my formlessness, my boyish smallness, and I sit with my hands to myself, folded in. I am not
yet married, though the man who will be my husband
stands nearby, and I am moody, reflective, an outsider, a
guest at a party of my future husband's friends. I spend my
time watching Robin's family, and it occurs to me, strikes
me hard at the end of the day, that the four of them are
what family should be: carefree and trusting, fingers
entwined. *I will aspire to that,* I say to myself, and the
thought settles in like resolve.

THE NEXT TIME I saw Robin, it was much too cold for that
time of year and far too wet to be stomping through a half-
built house imagining a roaring fire in the fireplace or a
garden out beyond the molten concrete pads. Nevertheless,
we were there—Robin, the architect friend, my husband,
and me. Yes, I was four years married by then. I was there
in that house with my husband, and I was holding the only
child we'll ever have.

Though I didn't know this part yet. What I knew was
that we had come to that place because my husband was an
architect, too, and because he and the mutual friend had
jointly brought this house to life in the woods, turning
drawings into stone. I thought it was a beautiful house, and
Robin seemed delighted; and even though her family
(which had grown to include another child, a son) had not

made the trip with her that day, I was confident—I knew—
that Robin would live happily in those woods.

In the house that day, there was work to be done and it
was raining, and I took my son to the mezzanine level,
where the windows already had their glass and the bridge-
ways had railings. Robin stayed downstairs and I watched
her from where I was. I remember thinking how remarkable she seemed, how much in command. She had energy
and ideas and she urged the contractors on with a woman's
wile—measuring the planes with an old-fashioned squar-
ing device and running her polished nails across the saw-
dust surfaces. "Buddy," she'd say to whomever was near.
"Plane that door one more time, for my sake." And of
course Buddy would, because a doll had addressed him, and
because nothing was denied Robin.

Later, the architects came in from outside, where they'd
been checking on grout. Robin was in front of the fireplace
by then, tapping the glazed bricks and smiling. "Not bad,
boys," I heard her say, though her back was turned to me.
She said that, and then the architects nodded, then they
traded high fives and proud smiles. The three of them did,
standing there near the hearth. So satisfied with the
strength of that house.

Still upstairs, I watched the celebration—a spectator
once again. It was Robin who remembered me first, and
with her free hand she gestured me down the stairs. I came,
climbing the steps in loud shoes with my son, clumsy in the
way that plank boards and small children can make one.

By the time I reached the bottom step, my son was sobbing, suddenly hungry for milk. But I was too shy to lift my
shirt in front of so many men, in front of Robin. Maybe she
guessed that. Maybe the noise of a hungry child in her

house provoked her. It doesn't matter. She chose to speak to me, directly, something she had never done before. "Give your whole self," she counseled, though it was milk that she meant. It was one mother to another, and I complied.

———

EVERYTHING ELSE I know about Robin comes on the strength of hearsay, from stories told about her and passed on to me. I learned how she had married young, settling down with her husband in a crowded college dorm. I was told she traded a degree for love, but no one questioned her authority. I was made to imagine how she did it all— cooked, mothered, wived, ran, powered a house right up out of the earth—and how she did it all like an unbounded spirit.

And then there was the story told about that third and unplanned child. She was nearly five months pregnant before she let on that she was. By then it was too late and there were complications and she was given no choice but to spend the remaining four months inside hospital walls, fighting her body's urge to empty itself of its burden. She spent the whole time on her side, away from her children, too far from her husband, unable even to read.

But her spirits, it was remarked about her, were never defeated. When it came time for the cesarean, Robin chatted pleasantly with the doctors. From behind the white drape, from above the hole in her skin, she asked questions about friends and careers, offered up construction advice, reported on running shoes, suggested (but with her body, she must have been kidding) that any fat stored up at the waist be excised along with child, placenta, and blood.

———

THERE WERE NO more Robin stories after that. Enough is enough, and besides, my husband and I had our own lives to live. There was our son, and things weren't going as planned. We had work to do. All that mattered, for a very long time, was that my husband and I clench our fists, love our child, and fight hard to survive. No lawn sprinklers, no sun decks, no fingers entwined. Just therapy, and huge hope, and prayers. Our eyes always looking for signs, looking for progress, our hearts always able to find it. Though our bodies grew weary and our lives grew small as the fists we were making. Our days lost their firmness, their measure.

It is therefore true that I had forgotten all about Robin, my admiration, my resolve. I had not thought of her, and so it shocked me, one night, when my husband came home with the news that Robin was gone. Packed up and left— her husband, her three children, her home in the trees—for a man she'd met fifteen years before in that crowded college dorm.

I pressed my husband for details, but he had no more to give. "That's it, that's all I know," he said. "Gone. No one has heard from her since."

EVER SINCE MY husband's revelation, Robin's disappearance has been at me; in me. When no one is looking, I give my energy to it. I shuffle the clues like a detective with a portmanteau of freeze-frames. I see the hands clasped. I see the children unbridled. I see the perfect nails inside the pine-board shavings. I hear the voice. In my mind's eye, I see Robin snapping the roots that had sustained her, and trusting her spirit to follow.

But how could she? I ask the question, and I believe it is valid. How could she, with all that she had?

It's a tricky business—indeed, it isn't my business—imagining the urge that broke through, the rope that tightened and snapped in a woman I know no better than once-read fiction. But I persist. I take it clue by clue. I don't let it go.

One cannot, with assurance, speak to the dynamic between a man and a woman, a husband and a wife. The horror, the engulfing horror, is the children. Leaving, as she did, those children: in mid-sentence, mid-mood, mid-becoming. I imagine her in their rooms that last night—pressing them with kisses, speaking the fatal final words, turning off the light, guessing the future. I imagine her taking in their odors—holding her breath, closing her lips, afraid to exhale, afraid of losing one small particle of them. I imagine the children. And I wonder how.

I wonder at me.

I think of myself and how, at age twenty-four, ten years ago, I began my pursuit of a rooting-in place: sun and soil. I had drawn a conclusion, I had made my resolve, I had sketched out the line of my life. I had wanted: a man loved. Children, mine. A modest home, a small circle of friends, a name steady and certain, days peeling off burning sweet as the rings of red onions. I had wanted to spend my days in the sun, fingers in fingers, children running naked through the yard. As if plans were somehow guarantees.

And yet—finally sprouted with family—I have found myself longing for wind. Ungraciously longing to be swept sparse and stemless through the storm of sky, to be dropped down rootless in a place I cannot name. Because a child cries and I cannot cure. Because the future asks and I do not know. Because I have talked too long, too insignificantly, and wish to be gone from my own smell. Because I can no longer hold the molecules of my life on the palm of my hand and make sense of the strange markings there.

I am guilty of it: I find myself longing for wind. To be borne off, free. To arrive at another destination, unknown. I am a mother, a wife, a woman at dawn, clenched and dangerous within herself, by herself, faithless with wondering, faithless with imagining, with wanting to know one thing only: What calms a woman in the midst of her storm? Is it the strengthening of roots, or is it flight?

Robin thought she knew; I never will. She drew a conclusion, followed her instincts, ripped herself out of the earth in a storm. But for me in this morning, at the break of this light, there is only one thing, and that is this: In the room above where I write, two sleep still—a husband, a son, together and apart, churning in their dreams.

In his bed, my husband is releasing fragments of Spanish to the air, remembering the jungle of his birth, considering the journey he did not think would end here. Even as he sleeps, he wonders.

In his bed, my son, my only child, is playing his hand like an instrument, turning his right foot around and around like the time on a clock, giving his whole body to the dream—snorting, wheezing, giggling, perhaps, amazed by and afraid of the night.

And I know that when he wakes, my husband will bring his body down to mine—surprised perhaps to find me here, but trusting. And when he wakes up, my son will be surprised by the language he finds. He will press his cheek against mine, in need. He will lead me by the hand to a park bench in winter, gather sticks to eat with and leaves for gruel, and show me how to sup like kings. He will remind me of how far he has come and how long the journey still is, and he will trust me to go the distance with him.

That, in this dawn, is all there finally is: two sleeping still, three restless hearts, one sudden, quiet knowing that these things I will not surrender, in the midst of this great storm.

working it out

*D*uring the fall and winter of the following year, we drive along a stretch of industrial roadway, onto a six-lane highway, and then down leafy backroads to a language-enriched preschool, where for two and a half hours in the afternoon twice each week Jeremy moves through free play, circle time, and arts and crafts under the tutelage of both a teacher and two pedigreed speech therapists. He has gained the strength and self-confidence to let me leave him, after the first several days, on his own. I don't go far; I walk around the school yard, let him know that I'm always there if he needs me.

I have established two goals for my son at this school: help him overcome the pronomial reversals that relentlessly nag at him and entice him into a more direct form of dialogue. At home Jeremy doesn't tell us what he wants or what he's thinking. He holds to his own strict policy of never asking any questions. I take some of the blame for this as his parent; in an attempt to model the pragmatic use of language, I have, whenever greeted with one of his unarticulated frustrations, tried to guess at the problem, then—retrospectively—given him the words he might have used to address it. I do not let his bouts of tears go on too long. Instead I'll ask him, *Do you want a book? Do you want the red book? Do you want the red book about the knights in armor?* When I finally manage to locate the object of his desire, I turn the language right back around. *Oh, Jeremy wants the red book,* I will say. *Jeremy wants the book about knights because he wants to read it. If I were Jeremy, I would have said,* I want this book. *That's what I would have said, because this is a neat book, Jeremy. I understand why you want it.*

Maybe I should be more forceful. Maybe I should not retrieve a book until it's properly asked for, but my gut tells me that the kindness in the house, the total rewriting of conventional rules, is paying dividends. More often now Jeremy tries to tell us about the things that he loves, gives little unprompted lectures on his fascination of the moment. To make sure I'm listening, he sometimes catches my eye, and though he steers clear of opinions and tries to avoid any subject matter that would require him to make a pronoun choice, it is a blessing to hear him put more and more words in a row. I have a clearer understanding of why pronominal reversals are so important, know that his confusion over *I*'s and *you*'s is slowing him down, getting in the way of what he'd like to tell us, and so, in my first entry in the journal I'll be sharing with his teachers, I make a note that correcting the pronominal reversals is our top priority.

Jeremy seems, through October and November, to be happy. He loudly hums the songs he's learning, tries to answer my questions about his afternoons at school with *yes*'s and *no*'s and *don't know*'s. Through the journal we get more information about the games he's playing, block towers he's building, snacks he's eating, and between the lines I try to discern what's being done about pronominal reversals. I recognize that there are subtle tools that specialists use, integrative therapy that might not easily be written down, but when I ask questions outright about the school's approach to pronominal reversals, I realize that there's nothing magical, nothing more than I'm doing every day at home. They're asking Jeremy *who* questions, just like I do, day in, day out: Who's Jeremy? *I am?* Who's Jeremy's mommy? *You are.* Whose hat is that? *It's mine.* Looking at photographs and saying, Who is that? *It's me.* Who is that? *It's you.* I allow myself the familiar disappointment that there is no secret code, no proven cure. It's a brief sensation. It passes. I'm getting used to the idea that it's not science that we're working with, but a little boy, our child.

A LITTLE BOY, who at the moment is enthralled with knights. The passion began with the simple enough gift of a Playmobil horse and its ribboned jouster, and it has multiplied quickly into a village of expensive plastic replete with drawbridges, moats, fainting ladies, reviewing tents, clutches of money, swords, feathers, tools of war. It is true that we have indulged our son, but this new obsession has been an adventure of sorts—cause to go out in the morning to the local toy store in search of a brand-new box of knights or a little magic, a fire-breathing dragon, a ball and chain, a pair of cannons, and then to stop at the library or bookstore for a handful of facts about round tables and kings.

While Jeremy has played busily on the floor—clicking the armor onto his men, snapping the swords into their hands, mounting the dignified warriors onto the sturdy backs of horses, framing the perfect rhythm of a march, raising the momentous castle door—I have lain on his bed and read out loud from the books: *Historical Facts: The*

Middle Ages. Knights in Armor. Crusaders, Aztecs, Samurai. Long Ago in a Castle. King Arthur and the Magic Sword. It isn't always clear which passages of language Jeremy hears, though at times he will stop and cock his head, then quickly rearrange his subjects according to the dynamic in the book. King Arthur and Sir Lancelot will go out hunting for fowl while Guinevere raises a sorrowful hankie from the balcony behind. Morgana and Mordred will hatch another terrible plot. Little Merlin will cast some sort of spell sending all the bad guys in town into a deep blue sleep. I try to draw lessons for Jeremy while I read him these books. Talk about values and priorities, heroes and villains, the things that—had they only been articulated by the hero in time— would have surely staved off disaster.

Other books have the power to lift Jeremy right off the floor and to my side. These are the textbooks, adult in both size and complexity, that lay out the facts of medieval times. This is where we learn, for example, that El Cid rode a famous horse, whose name was "Stupid." We read about cockatrice, that delicacy of the strange Dark Ages. We discover that the heavy iron gate to the castle was given the off name of *portcullis*. I practice saying the word, but I have no idea how to pronounce it, and I wonder if Jeremy feels disappointed in me. When I leave the room, Jeremy spreads out on his bed and studies these textbooks cover to cover.

❧

I CAN'T REALLY put my finger on a cause, but by Christmas Jeremy's lost interest in knights, and things are dissolving again. Without an obsession he's forlorn and empty. He gets tangled in his tasks at home. He forgets to look us in the eye. It doesn't occur to him to start a conversation. He gives fewer lectures. He's less engaged in what we're saying. At pickup time I learn that nothing much captures Jeremy's attention at his school. He's started drifting off at circle time, I'm told. He's displaying little interest in the other children. At recess he has taken to neither ball, bike, nor bridge, and during art he's impatient at the easel, disenchanted with scissors and glue, quick to toss the crayons onto the floor. We get the sense that a slow frustration is beginning to build on the part of Jeremy's teachers, and Jeremy himself has begun to exhibit greater resistance toward the school. He doesn't want to get in the car and go, and at the door to the school he clings to me with a genuine fierceness, won't let me go, looks back at me with tears in his eyes, tells me everything he needs to, without words. It's a setback: this was the one hurdle I thought we'd crossed in the fall.

At home we're making up the rules as we go along, and I know we're far from perfect. We're too quick to indulge in Jeremy's imaginary worlds. We're too easily drawn into the incandescent quality of his mysterious persona. We should be more vigilant. We should have more answers.

It's late January, and I'm growing uneasy. I begin to see how terribly I've erred—staking my son's entire well-being on a single school, only five hours a week. What was I thinking? He needs more than that and I'm losing time, but I'm incapacitated by the lack of true options. We have come to the best school we believe there is for the diagnosis he has received; we have paid the full tuition for the year.

I'm back on the phone. I'm back calling places that I previously dismissed, and then I'm dismissing them all over again. Same reasons, new reasons, it doesn't much matter. There are marvelous settings for autistic children, but the issues Jeremy is facing are not quite the same as those faced by those schools' children; it would be fair to no one to put him there, and besides, the school administrators don't extend an invitation. There is behavioral modification, forty hours of in-home, in-your-face therapy a week, and while this works beautifully for some—I read the books, talk to parents—I know intuitively that it is not right for us, not right for Jeremy and his gigantic imagination. There is a private preschool that advertises its acceptance of "special" kids, but when I explain Jeremy to the headmistress, when I drive there, Jeremy in tow, and submit to an "interview," I'm told that my son is not special enough. "We have a bias toward those with the kind of physical handicaps that the other children can readily see," the headmistress tells me point-blank. "Those sorts of handicaps are easier both to remember and to be kind to, and what we focus on here is empathy. Your son, his difficulties, are—to the young eye—invisible. He wouldn't be of much use to us here."

I make phone calls and more phone calls. Two days a week I take Jeremy to school, pace the parking lot, drive him home. One morning a week I drive him to an occupational therapist, where I sit mutely on the interior steps of her done-up-for-business house and watch as Jeremy pushes a yellow ball up a slight blue incline, as he hangs—petrified—from the ceiling in a swing, as he tries to draw with stencils, as he hammers a wooden toy to its death, as he jumps from letter to letter on an alphabet floor, but not on one foot, as he has been instructed. The rest of the time it's just Jeremy and me and whatever I can intuit, and in the night I worry. I am not doing enough, I feel it intensely. I am not taking care of my son.

IT IS OUT of sheer desperation that one day I take down the phone number of a rather new nursery school up the street. It's housed in a church that was previously a restaurant, and before that who knows what purpose the lumbering white building served. OPENINGS STILL AVAILABLE is all the sign promises, and then a number, which I dial later that night. I've obviously connected with a residence—a child answers, then calls for Mom, and then I listen to the corrupted noise of a distant TV while I wait for the woman to come to the phone. She's laughing when she gets there, makes some inside joke about dinner for five, and then gets around to me: "Why did you call?" she asks, still laughing at something, and I'm so thrown, so used to talking through a choke in my throat to a hovering authority on the other end of the line, that all I get out at first is, "I saw your ad for a nursery school. I dialed the number."

"New Life Nursery," she says. "We think it's a pretty neat place."

"Why?" I ask her. The word slips out before I realize how odd the question must sound.

"Well," she reflects, her voice still open and weightless, "I think we have pretty neat teachers. They're all trained and certified, of course, but our first criteria is that they genuinely love kids."

"Oh," I say. I almost ask, *What kind of kids?* but I catch myself in time.

"And then there's the activities we do. This week we are visiting Morocco."

"Morocco?"

"I lived there," the voice says. "So I've got the outfit and the maps, and we talk about customs and foods. That's circle time. And then we've got really fun crafts, all tied, you know, in some way to the letter of the week, and we've got big bags full of dress-up clothes and a corner in the back that's full of cars. For the boys, you know," she says. "Some boys love cars."

"Oh," I repeat. I listen intently. The head of the New Life Nursery School doesn't suspect why I have called, what sort of mother I am, what I am fearing. I let her go on as long as she possibly can, strain to learn something from the carefree quality of her voice.

"So you have children?" she asks, after a while.

"One," I say.

"And he's . . ."

"Three and a half. He'll be four in July."

"A great age," she says. "We have great kids in that group."

"My son's pretty great," I say.

"Sure," she agrees. "Aren't they all?"

"He's pretty great," I say again, because this, above all else, is true; the problem lies in learning how to reach him, in finding the best place for him, in giving him a shot at regular little boyhood. But can I explain that now? Can I begin that conversation at this hour, on this day, at this moment, when maybe I won't have the words that work?

"Uh-huh. Well, tell me about him. Tell me why you called." The woman is patient, but to the point. There can be no more stalling.

"Great because he's gentle," I start. "Great because he creates these landscapes in his mind and finds a way to walk through them. Great because . . . you'd have to see him. He's very different. He exudes this incredible quality."

"Terrific," she encourages. "And you called because . . . ?"

"Actually," I say, "I called because I have a question to ask you. Called because, well, in fact, I'm wondering: Are you open to taking on children with special traits? Are you

. . . Do you have any problem with that?" I get it all out in a single breath, then I slouch back, bite my lip, and wait.

"We tend to think that all kids are special," the woman remarks, after a moment. Maybe her voice sounds different; I don't know. I hear the TV. I hear children behind her in a mild tussle. I hear a father's contravening voice. "How would you describe the specialness of your son?"

"My son——" I start.

"Whose name is . . . ?" she interrupts.

"Is Jeremy," I tell her. "Jeremy."

"I love that name," she says supportively. "I also think the world of Jeremiah."

"Jeremy, like I was saying, is an incredible little guy." I want to get on with things now. I want to get through this and on to the next thing.

"I bet."

"Intelligent, kindhearted, gentle, an imagination the size of the sea. Jeremy is all those things."

"It's an amazing age," the head of New Life encourages. "The things they come up with."

"He's also quiet," I say. "Very quiet."

"Shy?"

"Extremely quiet. And he puts inordinate emphasis on just a few spare things."

"Like?" the woman wonders. I feel pressure, a little. I'm trying to get to the point.

"Cars," I say, as if that could explain it. "He loves cars. Also trains. Until recently he was enamored with castles."

"Cars were big at our house for a while," she tells me. "My son is four."

"See," I say, my voice too loud at this point to be considered conversational. "My son received a diagnosis from a children's hospital more than a year ago. Pervasive devel-

opmental disorder not otherwise specified. We're still not
sure what it means, entirely, or whether those are the right
words, or what the future is; best as we can tell, PDD is
merely a category, a grouping of traits for kids who struggle with language, motor skills, social awareness. We've had
him in individualized therapy, and in a special summer
camp. He's enrolled right now in a speech-enriched school.
I take him to an occupational therapist. But my heart tells
me that it's not enough. My gut says that his social development is at an impasse; something has to be done. I'm
starting to think that what my son needs most of all is just
a regular, everyday preschool. A place he can go that accepts
him for who he is, protects him where he's vulnerable, but
most of all prepares him for the world as it is." I stop and
catch my breath. I wonder if I've said too much. Have I
been clear? Have I violated my only child's privacy? "What
I think he needs," I add clumsily, "is to see regular kids at
regular play. Just to observe them for a while, until he's
comfortable joining in. I think he needs that right now. I
think he does."

"We're not trained therapists," the woman tells me, after
a pause.

"I know," I say quickly. "I'm not looking for that."

"We have a one-teacher-to-eight-students ratio. One-on-
one attention around New Life is rather catch-as-catch-
can."

"I don't expect that," I say. I lay my head back on the
floor where I've been sitting and stare at a ceiling of webs,
signs of a house that's gone untended for what seems years.
I blew it, I think. I said too much.

"Jeremy sounds like an interesting child." The head of
the school sounds contemplative despite the low rumble of

the TV behind her. I try to picture her face, but it's elusive.

"He's incredibly sweet," I tell her truthfully, lifting myself back up onto my elbows. "He's not disruptive. His heart is gold. But he's deep inside himself. He needs the company of friends. He needs an environment like the one you've described. He needs—I don't know what he needs." I sound like I'm begging. Or like I'm trying to talk myself into something unreasonable. Or persuade this woman who, until minutes ago, was nothing to me but a stranger.

"If Jeremy is comfortable here . . ." the head of New Life offers after a long considered pause. "If you are, too . . . if you're comfortable . . . then maybe we can find room for him here. We should meet, of course, ahead of time, and I recommend a gradual introduction to the classroom."

"Whatever it takes," I say. "Really. We'll give it a try." Relieved beyond words, I find that my eyes are welling. I didn't realize, when I made this call, that I was going to want New Life so badly.

"We need to be honest with each other," the woman cautions. "If it's working or not working. It doesn't help anyone to skate past the truth."

"I know that," I tell her. "Really."

"I'm glad you saw the sign and called," she says, her voice regaining its original tone. "Ring me tomorrow. We'll schedule a meeting. We can take this as fast or as slow as you want."

⤚

IT SEEMS TO work, though it's definitely hard at first, me again chaperoning Jeremy through preschool paces, me waffling through moods of excessive optimism and unprovoked despair. Since Jeremy has a late summer birthday, we have the option of placing him with children who are slightly younger or older than he is; we choose the former, thinking it will give Jeremy time to catch up.

Occupying as it does the lower chamber of this former restaurant turned church, New Life Nursery is organized around a sociable corridor, with the youngest children (two years old) located in the rooms nearest the glass exterior doors and the oldest children (prekindergarten) in the rooms at the opposite end. The white cinder-block hallways are decked out with the themes of the week, interesting photos, the work of the young, faded poster board. The teachers wear smocks and for the most part ponytails, and the appearance of slight disorder is in some ways calming. Play, not serious business, is the first priority of this school, and Jeremy seems to sense this, seems to relax—sooner than I could have hoped for—into the mild routines of the three-day-a-week, three-hours-a-morning program. True, he sometimes sits with his back to the circle during circle time, and yes, he's found a corner that he favors. But he'll remain at the table during art time and he'll experiment with the wooden indoor slide. And after the first several weeks, he seems to have lost all nervousness, not to care whether I'm with him, and I begin to leave him to his own devices and walk home, spend an hour by myself. Come back earlier than the mothers are due so that I can watch for signs of progress through the door.

We are blessed to have Miss Janie at the helm. We are blessed, too, to have her son Timmy, whom Jeremy, after a length of time, appears to notice out of the corner of his eye. Timmy is yellow-haired and intense, imaginative beyond his years. He likes the same bucket of plastic toys that Jeremy favors, and more than once the two of them have tangled in a shared fantasy. I try not to make too much of this; the official term for their arrangement is parallel play. But it affects me beyond words to see my son sitting down with another on the floor of a normal preschool, and even that is not all that there is. Two or three months after we've been enrolled in the program, Miss Janie offers to take Jeremy to her home. We know each other well by now. I know that she will know what to do. I trust her, and so does Jeremy, and it's not baby-sitting exactly that she's offering, or a casual trip to a playmate's home. This is something much bigger than that. A tug on a too-long-locked door.

But I know, despite all this, despite what is good here, what might be changing, I walk on dangerous ground. I have taken Jeremy's future into my own untutored hands, opting out of a classroom full of therapeutic interventions so that I can place him on a much quieter path. It's an odd way to achieve aggressive goals or stimulate those precious neural pathways, and I'm swimming against the tide— risking Jeremy's future, some would say, wasting another stretch of time. But I press on. Something intuitive whispers, *Trust your son.* And now and then when he looks up at me, I stare, as hard as I can, into those great round eyes and see what I have to see there: the small signs of healing.

houseguest

Gaps, of course, remain, though if on some days I can articulate just what they are, more often now Jeremy's difference is indistinct—a presence, not a suite of hard facts. I know, for example, that a child Jeremy's age should run to the door when company comes knocking, or at least not tremble at new faces, or at least not make it almost impossible to have guests. Another child his age might notice the phone when it's ringing, might take an interest in Disney movies, might experiment with contrivances and antics. He might nag his mother more, ask prickling questions, take an aunt or uncle by the hand and say, *Look what I'm doing. Don't you want to play with me? Don't you? Please look.* Might say his words but once, instead of replaying the same sentence repeatedly, might have several things that interest him and not just one. And perhaps another child would not sing his way into the night, wouldn't be forever tumbling about in bedsheets, wouldn't pummel the bedroom drywall with his flailing feet, his fists that mean no harm. But Jeremy—well, Jeremy is not another child, and he does have his own agenda, and he is indeed often up far past midnight, drumming the wall with the flats of his feet and singing songs of his own complex making. It's not because Jeremy's angry or because Jeremy's being selfish. It's just that Jeremy is who Jeremy is, and I've gotten so used to his mysterious essence that I'm even less competent than I once was to evaluate him against routine measures. It's when I see Jeremy at Miss Janie's house or Jeremy at school or Jeremy at the playground that I remember—a stabbing insight—both that he's a very unusual child and that he's making remarkable strides.

By the time June comes and the school lets out for summer, he's ready to spend a few hours each week at Miss Janie's, whose three sons seem to adopt Jeremy as a fourth brother—share their peanut butter with him, their milk, their toys, their mom. Going to Miss Janie's is, for Jeremy, more like going to school than it is like hanging out at a friend's; there are the toys to explore, some structured craft-and-project time, a trip to the neighborhood playground, opportunities to see other kids at play, Miss Janie's very careful oversight. I am thrilled that Jeremy has a place like Miss Janie's to go to, and nothing is more satisfying than to arrive at pickup time—shoes everywhere, boys being boys, Jeremy looking comfortable with one toy or another, his socks hanging down over his toes. *No problems*, Miss Janie will tell me. Or, *Gave me a big hug today*. I try to picture that, imagine Jeremy giving Miss Janie a hug—is it a spontaneous gesture of his heart?—and then I hug him myself, whisper into his ear that he's growing up quickly on me.

~

To supplement Jeremy's trips to Miss Janie's, we introduce another round of speech therapy. We find a traveling therapist with a wonderful reputation who agrees to work right in the house, and on the day of her first appointment,

I clean the front rooms, sit Jeremy down, and begin explaining that we'll soon be hosting a guest. "She's bringing toys," I tell Jeremy. "She's really neat. You'll get to play a whole hour with her."

"No," Jeremy shakes his head. As in, no thank you. It doesn't matter what he says. His words will forever be music to me.

"I'm going to be right here with you," I promise him. "Playing and learning, too." I'm not sure how much of a selling point that is, but I intend to tell the truth. The curl of an eyelash gets caught in the fringe of his bangs. I straighten the strands and kiss his forehead.

"No." He's declarative and opinioned, and for the time being, he'll have his way. There's still a half hour between now and the time the therapist has planned to arrive, and I have no intention of unnecessarily upping the ante. All I really hope to accomplish with the therapist's first visit is to neutralize, if only slightly, Jeremy's antagonism toward houseguests. I steel myself for Jeremy's distress, steel myself against hoping for too much, and now I let Jeremy go upstairs and play with his cars, give him some time in his own comfort zone. Twice I call to him from the bottom of the stairs. "Ten more minutes, little guy." "Five more." I have absolutely nothing to do. I'm just watching the clock and calling out numbers.

At the scheduled hour I look outside and see the therapist making her way across the street. She seems every bit the modern-day Mary Poppins, encumbered, as she is, by carrying cases and plastic bags, big-handled department-store bags. She has a bulging canvas bag strapped over her shoulder and a stuffed, unzipped duffel bag she drags along the walk. She and I have talked at length about Jeremy's fear of visitors, we both expect this first session to be a challenge, and I love her already for having thought to bring so many toys. Something in one of these bags has to work.

Opening the door, I help relieve the therapist of her load, and then she stands in the living room while I explain that Jeremy has retreated upstairs. "We'll be fine," she tells me encouragingly, and before I go to retrieve my son I walk the therapist through the few small rooms of the first floor. We agree that the dining room would serve us best in terms of therapy; we can seat Jeremy in his high chair that way, make it difficult for him to slip away.

While the therapist gets organized, I find Jeremy, who is lying on his bedroom floor watching a stream of cars not go by. I wonder if the matchbox cars appear life-size from that close-up perspective, wonder what spins and stops and glistens and fades in Jeremy's intricate mind. "Little boy, our friend is here," I tell him gently. I get down on the floor and slowly lift him up to me. He stiffens and strains to keep his vision on the cars. "Jeremy, you should see the bags of toys she's brought," I continue. "It looks like she's lugged Santa's entire workshop down from the North Pole."

Slowly I bring myself to my feet and walk Jeremy out of his bedroom. He doesn't cry, but I do feel his heart against my chest, thumping and thudding too quickly. I know how scared he is, how anxious to have someone new in the house, someone who may not, I know he's thinking, understand all the rules of what goes where and what cannot be moved. Someone who might talk too loud. Someone who might get too close and expect some talking from him. The only people who ever come to the house these days are my parents, whom Jeremy adores, and my next-door neighbor and her youngest son, both of whom have earned their place in Jeremy's small book of trustworthy friends. All

other outsiders are unpredictable and therefore frightening, and because language doesn't come easily to Jeremy, he
has few defenses, in such circumstances, tends to hole himself up until the guests are gone. Today my son is being
very brave. He is facing one of his terrors, and he's not crying. More and more, he's a lesson in courage.

By the time Jeremy and I reach the dining room, the
therapist is ready. Her bags are lined up in sequence on the
floor; she's placed a few particularly intriguing items, some
with wheels, upon the table. Jeremy doesn't know what to
think, but then the fascination of all those toy bags begins
to win him over. Bypassing the therapist, dismissing greet-
ings altogether, Jeremy plops down beside a bag and takes a
peek inside. "Isn't this amazing?" I ask him. "Do you want
to play with some of these?"

Jeremy doesn't nod, nor does he refuse to be seduced. I
gently lift him to his chair. The therapist knows what she's
doing, doesn't push anything on Jeremy right away. Giving
him time to get adjusted, to pick and choose a displayed toy
without instructions, she looks at me across the table and
says, "He really is gorgeous." "I know," I say, never modest
about my son. There's no disputing how beautiful he is.

Jeremy plays some more, drives some of the wheeled toys
across the table, and slowly, very slowly, the therapist begins
to enter his world, ask him questions, think her own
thoughts out loud. "I like the guy in the red car, don't you?"
she confides conspiratorially with him. "I think he's the
best." *Vroom,* she drives. *Vroom, vroom.* "Geez," she asks
Jeremy, "where's this guy going?" She drives her car around
the town, mutters to herself about the need for groceries,
the need for gas. "Oh my goodness," she says, "I forgot to
mail that letter."

Jeremy steals a quick look at me as if to say, *Is this for real?* and then he starts driving his car after the therapist's car, passing in the passing lane, parking where the therapist parks. So far he hasn't said much—he's been gnawing on his thumb—but the color has returned to his face, his body is not nearly so tense, and he is engaged, and if this is all we get out of the hour today, I'll be ecstatic. Somewhere, I hope, in the back of Jeremy's mind, the concept of *guest* is permutating.

But the therapist doesn't stop after her first achievement. After a while she's got Jeremy involved in a naming game. From her bag of tricks she's pulled a deck of picture cards, and Jeremy is going through each one, labeling everything he sees. He's always loved this game, excelled at labeling pictures in books, has, in fact, a huge and impressive vocabulary that he enjoys exercising like this. It's putting the words into sentences that can get Jeremy stumped, organizing the language for its pragmatic purposes, and now, with the next game, this difficulty is underscored as Jeremy is asked questions about what he does when he's cold, what he does when he's hungry, why it's so important that he learn to brush his teeth—one of the many domestic conventions we've still not mastered; for the sake of his teeth, I'm his own private hygienist. It's harder for Jeremy to make the verbal connections, to answer the questions he's been asked, to see any point at all in learning to brush his own teeth, since his mother will do it. He doesn't like the game very much, loses focus. Five minutes go by and he stops trying altogether, makes it clear that he wants out of the high chair. There are just ten minutes left before the session is through, and we grant Jeremy his wish, release him, tell him good-bye as he runs back up the stairs. "He's wonderful," the therapist tells me. "We have a lot to work with here." She explains that some of the games she just played were actually tests in disguise, and she moves me generally through what her process will be over the next several sessions—she'll work on pragmatics; she'll work on response time; she'll work on parallel play, then cooperative play; she'll want Jeremy to eventually bring his own toys to her, actively share them, learn not to mind if things get shifted around.

I marvel at the therapist's ability to see so far ahead, deeply appreciate the confidence and enthusiasm with which she speaks about our future. I also reflect that much of what she's done reaffirms the patterns and approaches my husband and I have already started taking—speaking our thoughts out loud so that Jeremy can hear how we arrange them, engaging in his world so he'll enter into ours, giving him tasks he can perform before edging into tougher terrain, praising him only, providing no negative feedback, not pressing too hard when it's clear he's reached his limit. She's making the learning fun and not intimidating. She's presented herself as a friend and not as a therapist. She has enjoyed our son, seen his light, gotten excited. I can tell by the way she's speaking with me now. "So," she says, "same time next week. I'm really looking forward to it. I had fun today."

"So did we," I say. "Thanks so much."

"Listen," she says, her toy bags now reassembled, affixed to shoulders, to hands; the duffel bag is on the floor. "Next time I come, see if you can get Jeremy to open the door. Let's put that down as one of our goals."

"Sure," I say, "perfect," as I hear Jeremy above us, settling back down into the mechanical world of his cars.

waiting for the red baron

Jeremy and I, we're playing planes. It's his new favorite game, after all. "See?" he tells me. He spreads his arms out wide on either side, crooks his elbows, presses into flight. *Meeewompff*, his mighty Double-Wasp engine takes to the sky, flies faster than a Zero, wheels and dives. I sit below Jeremy, my knees to my chin. "Whistling Death," he says, grinning down to where I am, secure in his cockpit. "The F4U Corsair." I nod. He shows me wings that bend.

It's a daytime mission. Jeremy hunkers down and lands. Then my only child rises up again, makes his elbows straight, slants his body, speeds. "Four propellers," he says, though he is sure that I've already seen them. "Ten Brownings. Emerson nose." I shake my head, back and forth: negative. He forgives, then relieves me. "It's the Liberator," he says, still flying. "The big banana boat."

It is December. Jeremy is four. The sun brings no heat where it falls. I rub my hands together, warm my knees, stomp the cold out of my feet, tighten the strings on Jeremy's jacket to enclose his head in its hood. Jeremy will not wear this jacket next year; it is almost too small for him now.

"Guess, guess, guess," I hear him say, and I do look closely, try, though his arms, straight out, are no different than before. "Striped like a zebra." Jeremy is generous with clues. "Medium bomber. Four-bladed Hamilton Standards." I wish, as I have always wished, that I had been brought up a boy. Then I make my admission. "I don't know this one, either," I say. Jeremy takes me in stride. "The Marauder," he explains, lips pressed together like a schoolmarm's. Then he hardens his jaw and the lines on his brow to take the plane higher, so high.

I watch. I see how far he goes without moving. I feel myself filling with wonder. Then I cast my eyes around, collect my bearings. We are eight feet up, Jeremy and I, on a platform in a playground he has always called Orchard. Though that's not its name. It's the Harry Renninger Municipal Playground—a few trees, a weak creek, predictable structures for play.

"It's cold," I say to Jeremy. I stomp my feet again for effect, make white bursts with the air in my lungs. The weather makes no difference to Jeremy. It never does. He flies more planes. They rumble overhead: the Flying Fortress, the Lancaster, the Invader, the Mitchell, the TBF Avenger. His nose is turning red. "Cold," I say. "Brrr." We are alone in the playground. Jeremy likes it this way.

World War II fighters, the cold: they are but diversions. They are the prelude. What brings us to Orchard in December is another war, another force, another tradition Jeremy plays out every day: Manfred von Richthofen. He's so famous, even I have heard the tales. World War I. The Fokker Dr 1. Red paint. Downed twenty-one planes in one bloody April, killing the observer-gunners first, then the pilots. So methodical, he sifted through wreckage for souvenirs.

It occurs to me that I want nothing to do with the Baron

today. "Should we go home?" I ask. "No home!" Jeremy says. It was silly even to try. "Ten minutes," I say. Sometimes it works when I explain it that way.

Jeremy is a Mustang, Jeremy is a Mosquito, suddenly Jeremy nose-dives for me. He's in my lap. He hushes. I lean all the way forward, past his hood, to see his face. "He's coming," he says, his huge eyes skyward, his voice reverent. "Who is?" I ask, though of course I don't need to. "The Red Baron," he says. Jeremy only moves lips, he's so quiet.

I follow Jeremy's looking up through the blue, up through clouds. He is staring far away at a rumble he hears. It's silence to me, but Jeremy has extraordinary ears, an extra sense, a genius, though his doctors give his gift another name. He holds his breath, he is shivering with joy. I distract him with words, so he'll breathe. "Jeremy," I say. "Jeremy." "He's coming," he says. "This time he is." I notice the sun again, how it casts its light but brings no heat. I do not disagree with my son.

I remember my first lie. I am five. I am on the wrong side of the classroom, away from the windows, away from the sun, which I am sure is hot, if I could just touch it. The teacher yammers at the front of the room like a Charlie Brown adult, no words. I press my body toward where the sun is. I make a diagonal lean and hear, outside, the pitching shrill of an emergency vehicle passing by. I hitch a ride on the back of the sound, go with it, arrive, in my mind, to a roaring blaze, a fire, water through nozzles, fierce spray. *What did you learn today?* my mother asks later, warm cookies, the oak table between us. *Emergency sounds*, I say. *How to tell before seeing what they are.* Then I sit at the kitchen table pushing wind out my nose and mouth. *That's an ambulance*, I say, after a long whine. *That's the police.* Then I howl and howl until the sound hurts my nose—

burns it, going through. *The Woodbine Fire Protection Troop,* I say. *The sound of the number two engine.* My mother watches me carefully. She makes a low whistle, then pushes her chair back hard against the linoleum floor. She slips out of the room, leaving me out of breath with the lie. Even now, even today when a fire engine passes by, I remember.

"Jeremy," I say, "it's getting cold." But Jeremy can't hear me, can only hear a sound far away. I try not to imagine how long this will take, how long we'll stay shivering here on a splintered platform alone, waiting for the Red Baron to come. I get a quick flash of nights, days, weeks.

"I will tell you a story about the Red Baron," Jeremy says, and he does. He lists achievements. "He could land a Halberstadt. He could land an Albatross. He could shoot down FE2s. He could lead a *jasta.* He was the head of the great flying circus."

"Mmm," I say, nodding to the chant I've grown accustomed to. I could counter with the truth. I could say: *He put bullets into his own grandmother's ducks at ten. He hunted the ghost of a tortured man. His eyes were pale instead of blue, he lagged behind the others in school, and he wasn't immune: he took a shot in his own head—a four-inch wound that showed skull, splinters of bone, fear.* I could tell Jeremy things that are true, but then I lean forward again, look in his eyes, see with what respect, what love he views the skies, and I go silent, shiver, gather him next to me, close. I do not speak. I am my son's accomplice. We are waiting for the Red Baron to come.

I remember my second lie. I am eight years old, behind a closed door. It is my mother's sewing room. There are scissors, silver shears, and my sister—four years younger than myself, Jeremy's age—is sitting on the sewing stool, patient and trusting, long flyaway hair. I tell her I will fix her strands, and I mean to, but the scissors keep cutting in the wrong direction, keep demanding a fix. The hair falls longer and heavier on the floor, shorter and jumbled on the head, and the scissors keep making their slicing sound, won't stop, though my hands tell them to. Later, my mother keeps asking, *What did you do? What did you do?* All I keep saying is, *Nothing. Nothing,* I say. *Nothing. It wasn't me. Nothing.* I stare straight into my mother's eyes, and once more I say it: *Nothing.* She shakes her head, ashamed for my sake. Then she says nothing more, takes up the shears, and gently straightens the tiers on my sister's shorn head.

I wish I had remembered gloves. My hands are so cold now, they look like bone, feel brittle to me, when I move them. Jeremy's hands protrude from his jacket, and I cover them with mine—numbly find and curl around them. I lean forward again, past the hood, press my cheek against his, though I can't find the touch of his skin in the cold. His breath warms the air in front of us. He whispers to me, saying, "This time the Red Baron will come."

I wonder how Jeremy sees. I wonder if right now, all around him, there is battle smoke, downed enemy planes, the roaring sirens of death. I wonder if he sees a red speck in the sky, hears the feathered propeller of a sputtering Fokker, is watching British Camels and Bristols flip upside down and loop. I wonder if any of what I see—the sewage creek, the broken spires of the trees, the hard iced sky— passes through his sight as well. I wonder just what vision is, and how a mother forms and guides it.

It is the constant question. It is the other voice inside my head. Ever since I was told there was something different in my son, I have felt—depending on the day—astonishment, despair. Expect obsessions, the doctors said. Expect cataloging, repetitions, fantasies, an aversion to ordinary circumstance, a different way of seeing. Expect these things, then fight them off: each one. Break them until a tree is a tree and a sky is a sky. Break them, or run the risk.

After the bullet tore a hole in his head, Manfred von Richthofen was an altered man, his taciturn nature gone black and melancholic. He began counting the dead pilots who had been his friends—obsessing, it was said, retreating. He was tired. He was disheartened. His head pounded like a heart out of place. War had consequences, and he, for the first time, was seeing.

Following the hospital, the surgery, the intensive care, he went home to the woods of Schweidnitz to rest. There he wrote his autobiography for the German propaganda machine and sought solace from the pistols, the goggles, the flying caps, the photographs, the altimeters, the silver he had stripped off dead men. He ran his finger down a wall of wartime medals and tried, desperately, to retrieve his old way of seeing, to believe again that he ruled supreme: that skill, not luck charted futures. He saw himself in a cockpit of fire instead, writhed with the conjectured pain of it, smelled, thought he did, the fumes of his own skin, ascending.

The sky is cold blue, like lapis crying. "Mommy, Mommy, Mommy." The word hangs in the air—a white burst—then is dispersed. "Yes, Jeremy?" I answer. "It's the Red Baron," he confides. "I know he's coming." I press my ear up, do not detect a drone, do not detect anything more than the sky. "I don't hear him," I say, and then I check myself. "Perhaps he's on the ground still, refueling."

One lie is all you need and you're over the threshold. I knew this even as a child. That's why it became easier, over time, to lie to my mother. Never harmful deceits, never evil constructs, just big, impressive stories that made me larger and more noble, braver and more interesting than I ever in fact was. It got so that all that mattered was how grand the stories made me. It got so that all I ever wanted was for my mother to look up from her sewing, her wonderful cooking, her books, and not see the ordinariness of me.

Manfred von Richthofen went back to the war not telling a soul that he had grown frightened. Doubt is the first defeat, and Richthofen knew that if he showed the slightest tremor, if he grew skittish in the skies, the whole German people would be dealt a violent blow. So he multiplied their delusions, he returned not speaking truths, he killed again and again though his whole body ached with the task and his heart, too.

The Red Baron is dead. I should say these words right now to my son. I should explain how it was when Manfred von Richthofen went down—the Fokker caught off guard, the Camel gaining speed, the Baron's tripe ripped apart in an explosion of bullets. In the end, his body slumped, his triplane warbled, he was hurled inglorious through a hailstorm of ground fire. He hit the earth. It didn't recede. He was just like any other man.

I should tell my son the truth. I should finish it, say that the Baron's corpse was stripped apart the moment it crashed down. They rushed at it wildly, in a frenzy: the Australian ground troops. They took his silk scarf, his monogrammed handkerchief, his boots. They made a skeleton of his plane, unscrewed the instruments, shredded his propeller into splinters. And when they were done, they tied his body to a sheet of corrugated steel and dragged it five miles over the ridge, a bloody sled.

Tell your son the truth, insist on the truth, break his patterns, his obsessions, his dreams. The doctors say this. Anything less, they say, and there'll be consequences.

The problem is, the reason I'm no good at this is that I'm afraid my boy will believe me. I'm afraid that he will see, the way he has a knack of seeing, the violent, shattering end. I'm afraid it will all go black for him and grim, that the skies, when he looks up, will be empty.

Or maybe he won't believe me. Maybe he will look out of those extraordinary eyes and see only a mother, nearly middle-aged, who has lost her capacity, her vision. He will look at me and feel disappointment, he will see me as regular, plain, and then he will turn to see what he dreams of, to watch the huge skies all alone. It is this—this threat of being ordinary and unseeing in my own son's eyes—that has become, I admit, my great fear.

"Jeremy," I say, shivering. "Little boy, it's getting dark." Because when I look around me now, it is—the tree limbs making black thrusts in the crisp and dimming sky. I am numb all over with the cold; my breath hangs in particles before me.

"Do you hear it, Mommy? Do you?" Jeremy asks the question, and suddenly, imprudently, I am fumbling with my fingers, untying his hood, throwing it back off his ears, so he'll hear more. "Yes," I say. "I do."

And that's when it hits me like a howl of thunder: a rumble from the north sky, a feathering, rapid commotion. Startled, I put my eyes to where the sound is—follow it, though there's nothing to see. "Jeremy," I say. "Jeremy."

"It's the Red Baron!" Jeremy is squealing, and then he is up on his feet, and I am, too, and maybe it's a star that far away, maybe it's a passenger plane, but something's coming. The platform shakes with Jeremy's jumping. The tree spires, the creek both recede. I throw my eyes up high. I wonder briefly if it is joy or confusion that I feel. "Can you believe it?" I say, though I don't know who I'm asking. "Can you?" And it occurs to me that it doesn't matter what happens next. It doesn't matter, for this single, suspended instant. We have seen the Red Baron, my child and I, and he is still flying high.

afternoon concert, minor keys

*T*he neighborhood freezes beneath a heap of winter, and Jeremy and I are alone. We have spent days like these, holed up inside with the phone not ringing, and we have made lists to keep us sane. 10:00 A.M.: bake cookies. 11:00 A.M.: straighten closets. 11:30 A.M.: remove the chicken from the freezer. Noon: roll Play-Doh into snake life on the kid-sized kitchen table, then fit those smarmy little snakes with clever little clay hats and slap on pink bow ties. Give them gooey little cars to drive, and take them for a ride; snake them across the linoleum table and screech at the top of your lungs. Do it right, it takes an hour. Do it wrong and you get bored, and you eat the cookies on the cooling racks, and you thumb your nose at lunch. Later, when you are again grown up, you clear the table of its clay and crumbs and serve up bottles of nothing—empty bottles that you and the boy will make brilliant with colored sand. Or you romp through a round of Candy Land or deal a hand of crazy eights, or you persuade and persuade the boy to play. It's good to have choices in winter.

Two o'clock, three o'clock, four o'clock are troublesome: Jeremy and I flip through French magazines, I steal a look at *People*, I feign sophistication while rifling through a book on Far Eastern art. Jeremy would give anything to go upstairs alone and watch his planes fly nowhere, his cars sit in their respective garages, his trains chug to a standstill, but I have pinned him to me; I am not letting go. Snow days especially, we must keep in touch, because there's no place to drive in this storm, no way to break obsessions once they start. "It's getting taller," I say to Jeremy, about the white stuff outside. And then I lay the books aside and cup my hand beneath his chin, cocking his head in another direction so that if he chooses to, he'll see the snow.

"Daddy?" he asks. Each of his syllables, every word that he says, is slow and drawn out, delivered with the careful precision of a foreigner.

"A few more hours," I say. "We still have plenty to do."

"Is Daddy coming home?" Jeremy asks, one word at a time. "Soon?"

I lean in toward him and feel the panic building in his chest. "It's okay," I tell him. "We're busy." I turn his chin again toward the window that is streaky and uncurtained behind us, and together we watch the snow fall, big frozen petals breaking off the sky. Jeremy is reluctant company, a captive in my arms, and I know it's once again up to me to fill the space between this hour, now, and Daddy.

❧

It's not a natural thing for me—to start a sentence before another's been spoken, to conjure up a question or two so as to make room for my own answers. But this is what I've learned to do, in all these years with Jeremy. I talk. Even though he's not amused. Even though I see him itching into the private corners of his mind, running a flapping finger or two in front of his eyes, so that he can better imagine whatever story he's telling himself beneath the cover of his mother's grating words. If I were not holding him close like this, he would be running in circles, grinding the carpet into premature old age, and saying, in words I'm only starting to comprehend, *Leave me alone. I see a movie in my mind.* He would be completely fulfilled and otherworldly content, and so my strategy and defense is to hug him too hard while I leaf through the pages of my mind, looking for a chapter that I have not read recently. "We could talk about kites," I say, out of the blue. "Or I could make up characters. You choose."

"Nothing," Jeremy says. He squirms his chin out of my hand and flickers his eyes everywhere except back into mine.

"But it's fun when we tell stories," I persist. "And it's not like we're going anywhere. It's snowing outside."

"Nothing," Jeremy pleads. "No stories. I want to be alone and play." I overlook Jeremy's stubbornness, and smile. There are no echoes in this house. The pronouns, after more than a year of hard work followed by an overnight conversion, are right.

"We *are* playing," I say. "Look." I nuzzle his nose and he pulls way back. "Okay," I tell him. "Free play in a few minutes. But first I'm going to tell you one story."

"One?"

"I promise." I have no idea what I'll talk about yet.

"One story. And then Daddy will come home?"

"Soon enough," I say. "Sure." I feel like the ugly girl in high school, the one I was. The one the boys confided in only when they wanted advice about their blond, arch-eye-browed heartthrobs. I am hideous and oversized, an outsider pushing myself into my son's imagination, imposing on him, saying *Let's be friends* to this child who's had his fill. But if we don't talk, I worry, he'll slip away. And talking, given Jeremy's mood, means delivering a monologue. On what? I don't know yet. I'm tired. I want to talk about a passion of mine.

➤

"MY STORY," I begin, "is about weather. Winter, like we're having now. I was eight years old, nearly twice your age, and I was living in Boston beneath snowdrifts."

Jeremy's fingers fiddle before his eyes. His stockinged feet are twitching.

"We were in Boston," I continue, "because Grandpop was going to school. Grandmom was there, taking care of the house. Uncle Jeff was my brother, like always, and Aunt Janice, same as now, was four years younger than me. She was your size, Jeremy. At one point she got lost in the snow. She collapsed inside a huge mound of it. We had to dig her out with a shovel."

I look at Jeremy to see if I've impressed him, but I haven't. His fingers are going wild in the air.

"Actually, we weren't living in Boston," I retract. "We were living in Needham, and there was a lake. One Saturday afternoon, in his new '69 Dodge Dart, Grandpop drove the five of us to that place."

"Was it a four-door?" Jeremy asks, suddenly alert, spontaneously casting his fingers aside for the moment.

"Yes," I answer. "Dark green."

"Did you have any other cars?"

"We'd sold a station wagon," I reply. "To get the Dart."

"Oh," Jeremy says. He starts with the fingers again.

"The lake was frozen," I go on. "The lake was . . ." I stop. "I don't know if you've ever seen anything quite that big before."

"Did it have paneling?" Jeremy asks.

"It was a Dodge Dart," I answer plainly. "It wasn't pan-eled."

"Oh." He's disappointed. He tries to squirm out of my hug, but I won't let him.

"The lake was so big that you could never get a complete view. Think about that, Jeremy. It was gigantic."

Nothing.

"So for a dollar or something, Grandpop rented us skates. And we all went out there on the ice—and we figured out, once we were one among many in that off-balanced crowd, that what had seemed smooth and pure from far away was in fact lumpy and pitted. Twigs were buried in the hard-ened water. Bugs and trash from summer campers were halfway surfaced. Lake ice isn't beautiful, like I had thought it would be. That was the first surprise."

"Is Daddy almost home?" Jeremy asks, twiddling. "It's getting darker."

"So do you want to know what the second surprise was?" I ask with an excess of animation, thinking the volume of my voice might turn his head.

"Almost home?"

I give him a cold stare, but of course he's not looking.

"Almost?"

"The second surprise was that I was a really good skater." I practically spit out the words. I stop, pause, refrain. "Like magic," I continue. "First I was fast. Then I was graceful." I'm exaggerating now, but I don't think it matters. "You know what a spiral is?" I show him with my fingers. "I could do one. You know about spread eagles?" I connect my feet at the heels and point my toes out in opposite direc-tions. "I could do that, too."

"Free-play time," Jeremy announces. "I want to go play with cars. I want Daddy to come home."

"I was a really good skater, Jeremy. Right off the bat." I have to fight off the arrogance I hear cropping up in my voice, the way I'm bragging just to win my son's heart. I feel a vague resentment toward my husband, the perpetual hero of a story he is not home to tell.

Jeremy says nothing. His fingers push at the air as if they're playing an invisible flute. With his head completely rotated on his neck, all I see is the blackness of his hair.

"After that lake in Needham melted, Jeremy, we moved. Grandpop was finished getting his fancy degree and we packed back up for his job farther south, but he promised me a trip to a rink. Indoor ice, Jeremy. A smooth white oval on a bunch of copper coils that was scraped clean, every few hours, by a machine."

"Was it a car?" Jeremy wonders reluctantly.

"More like a truck."

"Oh." More disappointment. The obsession with trucks is still a few months away.

"So guess what happened, Jeremy?" I ask, my voice tilted too high, like a circus barker.

Nothing.

"Guess?" I insist. I'm getting angry. *I'm your mother*, I want to say. *I'm giving my whole damn life to you. Can't you care, just a little bit, about my story?*

"You said just a few minutes of story," Jeremy reminds me. His feet are all out kicking now. "This story's too long."

"Well, that's too bad," I say. "Because I am going to finish." I pause. I take a breath. I wonder what all the other mothers in snowbound houses are doing right now. "Jeremy," I continue in the grip of a deliberate, lighter mood, "I was discovered. Yes I was. I was skating around on the public session and one of the stars of the rink happened to see."

Except for the wind at the window and the subtle smacks of wet weather against the glass, the house is terribly silent. "I was a good skater," I go on, remembering the feel of it. Remembering years after that first day at the rink, when I was an ice queen myself at the old scruffy rink at dawn—a crackling record on the phonograph player, the day's fresh light just filtering in. I owned my living then. I surrendered to nothing but the sound of the music that fell from the overhead speakers like slow snow. I was a skater crafting speed, cutting the ice, riding my edges. I was taking the corners wide, singing on short breath, driving my right knee, hurling my left, feeling the weightlessness, the upwardness, the long hanging cliff of height. Hanging, hanging, the bleachers spinning, me dropping down, and the ice would break into a thin white line beneath my blade. I was—I realize this now—completely free.

"Would you ever want to see me ice-skate?" I ask Jeremy, quietly, a hypothetical question. I feel vulnerable. I am desperate for him to nod and say yes, to take an interest in me, to validate my one obsession in life the way I've tried to validate his. I attempt to pull his eyes toward mine, but they are stuck far away and won't budge. "We could go to the rink here," I persevere. "There are rinks all over. I bet there are still jumps I could do. Footwork. I could show you what it's like to carry music on your skates. Dreamy and sad," I close my eyes and consider losses.

"What's ice-skate?" Jeremy asks impatiently, after I've let some quiet go by. "When is Daddy coming home?"

"Ice-skate," I answer, irritably. "You know."

"Is Daddy home?"

"Come on, Jeremy." I almost start my story again, a teacher giving a lesson, but something horrible snaps, some piece of me I didn't know was there, and I am at my son in an instant, throwing words all over the place, slapping the arm of the couch with my free hand. "Come on! What do you mean, 'What's ice-skate?'" I'm almost screaming. "What do you mean? What have I been talking about? Haven't you been listening? Ice-skating. Ice-skating! That was me, Jeremy! That was everything!"

"I want to play. I want to play. Let me go." Jeremy struggles; I hear his heart pounding too hard, too fast. Everything about him screams, *Leave me alone*. Everything about this instant tells me I am vulgar, insensitive, beyond the realm of language now.

But I can't stop. "Those cars, Jeremy. Those cars, they're nothing," I repeat. "They don't mean a thing. There's not a shred of truth inside them. Think about skating. Think about how free it could make you. *Think about me!*"

"My cars!" Jeremy hollers back. "Mine!" His sense of endangerment is all over his face, and suddenly, cataclysmically, it breaks my heart, this thing that I've done.

Except. I can't take it back. The words are said. I drop my face into my hand, ashamed, afraid of the unlocked rage in my blood. "I'm sorry," I whisper. "Really. I didn't mean it. Snow days are hard on Mommy, too."

"I want Daddy," Jeremy starts to cry. "I want Daddy. Daddy." He thrashes and kicks; I let him go, watch him run down the hallway, hear the echo of his footsteps up the thirteen stairs, hear him running the length of hallway above me, now through his door, now to the center of his room and all those frozen toys. I hear the weight of his body slump down to the floor and I know his mind is safe at last, at peace among his friends. No sound inside the house, and the light in this room changes abruptly, and the snow falls outside, pricks at the house, so many needles.

I STILL HAVE the music I skated to, the last year that I com-
peted on ice. The program had three sections, but the only
one that ever mattered to me was the slow, sad heart of it—
a gorgeous orchestral rendering of "Somewhere," from
West Side Story. I still know what my body did when that
music stretched before me, and sometimes now I'd give
anything to skate it, to inhabit the soul of that song.
Nothing feels like skating does. Nothing extends you and
frees you in that way, and nothing can make you as beautiful as blades on ice, as forgiving of the common structure of
your face or the insufficient body down below. To skate is to
mourn. It is to exult, and it is to seize eternity, to fracture
whatever it is that ties you down.

With words alone, I tried to give that to my son today, to
liberate him, the way I once was. Or perhaps all that I was
doing was filling vacancies, holding Jeremy at my side with
a strong arm and a long story. Or I was wanting his heart.
Proving: I am important. I am intriguing. I have something
to say. And I am not Daddy, and I am not trains, planes,
cars, but I am me, and there's something special in that.

Isn't there? Outside, the snow is brighter than the sky; it's
all I see now, pellets of white. It occurs to me that I haven't
heard the rumble of trains in the backyard, not for hours,
and that I don't know where my husband is, how close he is
to home. I never ask him anymore. There doesn't seem to
be time for the two of us. The only person I have any
knowledge of is upstairs playing, happier than he has been
all day.

I need to dance. I need the companionship of a song, the
metering of sound within time. I need to ache like music
does, and not like I do, like I have for so long now. I need to
be pretty, made transcendental by the mere, holy act of
extended, graceful limbs. "Somewhere" starts on long

notes. It falls, quickly, to edges. It leaps one time, and then it is a spiral down the center of the ice, a long spread eagle, a looping turn, an arc. It is my mother, in the bleachers, proud and genuine; it is the best double lutz of my life. *The snow can't go on piling up forever, can it?* I ask the leaden air in this room. And then I stand and sway in silence before the long, blank pane of glass, and listen for the sound of trains far off in the cold wet tunnel of winter.

competing wisdoms

*J*eremy stands at the front door, late winter, his feet
spread apart, his arms lifted high, his body stiff and
stretched as a lowercase x. "I want," he starts to say, and he
is facing outside, "I want," but the words won't come easily. Then it's like a cloud that's too heavy and breaks: "I want
someone, because Mommy, I'm lonely."

It's a word I didn't know Jeremy had, and it moans and
hovers above the black cushion of his hair. I am unable to
move, and then I run down the hall to the wide oak door,
where he is. "I'm right here," I say gently, and I reach my
arms out for him. But he stays in his x, stiff and panicked,
his eyes liquid in his milk-colored skin, his lips in a thin,
quivered line.

Two weeks later, we are in El Salvador: my husband's
home country, a reunion. It is the last night of this trip, and
we sit in the dark—my husband, his brother, and I. The
brother is speaking, saying of the child sleeping above our
three heads, "Why don't you give him a brother?" In the
black heat of the Salvadoran night, I feel the weight of the
question, the silence. "Look around," the brother says, and
his eyes are on me, not my husband. "Look at life. It's all
about brothers and sisters." And I hear the air move, break

like waves all around us, as my husband nods *yes* to his brother.

Six weeks later, the message comes through once again, at a reunion of cousins just outside D.C. My cousins are four women in their thirties, and they've had raw, burning lives, and yet they're laughing and giggling in phases. *What is it with you?* I want to say, but then I know what it is: they are sisters. They have carried one another over the hurdles of time. They have not been alone when it mattered.

⟶

I AM A sister myself, the second child of three, and so I say what I know to be true: it is a privilege sharing one's life with a sibling. Histories are richer, made grander. Memories that might otherwise fade survive. It is a gift, this lifelong companionship, and more often than not, parents give it. Other parents give it, but I will not.

Here it is, on this page: I am the mother of an only child who is destined, always, to be one. It's a failure of heart, not a failure of body. It is my choice alone, not my husband's.

Though I could blame it all on percentages. Sometimes I do, in fact, when people ask. I say that two and a half years ago, a doctor in a white coat and a whiter room meticulously confirmed what we perhaps already knew: Jeremy was different. There were signs of hope, but there were flags of caution. Nothing was certain, no prognostication could be made, the future simply could not be pegged.

And there was something else that was said that day, something buried in the bottom of the news: a second pregnancy would carry similar risks. A 7 percent chance, he guessed right out loud, that our next-born would face similar or even more challenging delays. The books I read in the aftermath confirmed that there was indeed a genetic link to disabilities such as his, though the strength of that link was hotly debated, with most researchers placing it closer to 2 percent.

⤜

NUMBERS HAVE A way of telling everything and saying nothing, and I'll be honest, they had no meaning for me that day. It was part of the blur, part of the enormous sadness, the bottomless disquietude that took us down, swept through my husband and me, as we sat in that room, hands not touching, dead white.

Afterward all I knew was that there was no time to lose and that it was my job to heal my son, help him find the parts that were missing. I took it as fate, and I sank my whole life into his—relinquishing therapy to therapists, trusting myself with everything else. Hours and hours of everything else. I did not mourn the loss of an unconceived child. I narrowed my focus to the living son, Jeremy.

What were the days like then? How did they go on, never seeming to stop and yet never really beginning? My body remembers. It counted, contains every hour. It knows that I would rise in the dark, early, and write. When the sky outside my window changed color, I would go upstairs and find Jeremy waking up, waiting, all black hair and big eyes and unspoken questions. *Hello, Jeremy,* he'd say to me as I walked through his door. Because that is what I'd say to him.

I would carry him to the room next door then, where his father was—expectant, also waiting. We would lie down, the three of us in that bed, not speaking to avoid the small echoes, holding hands. And that was sacred. That was silence. That was the breath of air that fed the day.

But of course my husband would soon have to leave—

there was his job to do, after all—and of course the words
would start, my words and then my words but coming from
Jeremy, and my son and I would begin to move through the
day—a gnaw of fear in my stomach, nerves, as if I were
performing onstage. We would move through Jeremy's
obsessions, through his fears, through all his toys set down
at implacable angles, through his slipping away—his body
horizontal on the floor, his hand rolling a miniature train,
car, plane back and forth and back and forth before the
deep wells of his eyes.

It was all about intervention, then, about taking the toy
away when Jeremy lost himself in it, about taking him out
of the house when he got lost in there, too, about inserting
myself into his world. It was about always pressing but not
too far, about driving to small rooms and their therapists. At
the end of the day, it was about lying in bed again, listening to Jeremy humming, not sleeping in the room next
door, and holding the hand of my husband, sometimes
explaining, sometimes not. My husband listened, pressed
for answers in his mind, tried endlessly to solve the Jeremy
puzzle. He grieved inside himself so that I could grieve out
loud.

I have to say that it wasn't easy. I have to say that the
weeks seemed endless and that friendships dwindled and
that what I considered my youth left me. I have to say that
there were wars inside me and fists pounded into the bed at
night, my whole body furious about what had not been
achieved. I feel compelled to say as well that I might not
have gone on had Jeremy himself not shown the way.

Jeremy's healing has been like tidewater—the warm
edge of the sea stretching in and retreating, the sound of a
rolling fury never far off. It has been all-engulfing and it
has been tempting—no, it has been necessary—to siphon

the world off, to give my son the whole stretch of beach on which to find his way.

Which means, and I know it's understood, that these have been lonely years—so lonely that at times I lost sight of my own solitude. I did not keep track of other families, how they were growing. I did not think about my own, about its smallness. I simply lived by my son, worked with my son, loved my son, counted the miles taken, guessed at the miles left to go.

—

JEREMY FOUGHT HIS demons with mind, wit, willpower, love. He fought his demons, and I took great pride in that. I took pride, and more than that, after two and a half long years of waging war against a genetic miscue, I began to find some peace of mind. I let my armor down, my guard. Little by little I let the world back in. I let myself believe that we were almost healed, that we all—the three of us— had earned our own lives back.

But you let the world in and you see things you were not able to see before. What I saw, little by little, was friends I hadn't seen for a while, friends who had somewhere along the way sprouted full families. I saw families at parks— four, five, six strong. I saw my own family: Thanksgiving Day, Christmas. I saw brothers and sisters, felt the weight of their equation.

And as the world infringed, as a semblance of normality settled in around my edges, I saw and felt the weight of another equation, too, a creeping and noisy statistic I had not taken time to consider before: one child, one gradua- tion, one wedding, one hope to ride the whole future on, one void when that child is gone.

Making myself busy with other responsibilities, I somehow survived, learned to not heed the growing clamor inside my head. But then, on a gray day in winter, late in a quiet afternoon, I stood in my hall and served as sole witness as my son stood at the front door of my house and called himself lonely because he is.

MATHEMATICS IS A tricky business, as I have said. The numbers refuse to have meaning. Because what does the sum of brothers and sisters mean when compared to a statistically minor risk? And isn't a small risk of disability the same as a huge shot at absolute ability? Isn't it all in the seeing?

Clearly, other parents take the chance. I read their stories, I seek them out. When I find them, the rare times that I do, I ask them point-blank in the middle of the day how they could dare to have two. "We weren't afraid," they say, simply enough. "We were not afraid of the challenge."

But that's just it: I am. I am afraid of trying again, of facing bad news again, of drawing the shades on the world while another child struggles against the cruel legacy of an unstable genetic mix. I am afraid of my own fears, of my own anguish in the night, of the possibility that a second child might not find his own direction, that my light might not be bright enough to help him find his way.

I am afraid of all these things. Not mathematics, not numbers, but fear.

Have another child, the world around me says. *Don't take the risk,* I say. It's the second voice I heed. And is it selfish? Is it greed? Is it intuition? Is it kindness? I don't know. I will never irrevocably know. All that I have is my son and the word *lonely* and all I can do is go forward.

On the days that it is warm, I take Jeremy to the park, where he plays. This year is different from all the other years: he makes his muscles work for him on the swings, on the rungs, on the boards, taking unspeakable joy from his mastery over equipment and acrobatics that fiercely frightened him before. "I can do this by myself," he tells me, over and over, forging a distance, insisting that I stand back, let him be. When I am far enough away, he calls, "I'm so proud," and flies. "I'm so proud." Because again he's breaking bounds. He's pressing limits. He knows that he can win.

I have to believe that my son will win in friendship, too. That he will find, in time, some one or two who will have patience when he falters (still too many obsessions, too many rituals, too much monologue, still a fear of intrusion in the house), so that they can take pleasure from who, at heart, he is: generous, affectionate, curious, wanting, in all things, to ascend.

In the meantime, Jeremy and I go to playgrounds. We go to libraries, bookstores; in the mornings he goes to school. He spends his time, if not precisely with other children, then near them—watching so that he can learn, circling close when he feels brave, practicing when he gets home the skill that most eludes him now: conversation. Jeremy upstairs in a clutter of Lego men, giving each plastic figure a voice so it will speak. Saying, "Hello, Timmy. Hello, Jeremy. Would you like to play?"

And me, downstairs, waiting, giving him the distance he has asked for, the room he needs to grow. Waiting and wondering, then hearing, suddenly, his voice falling down from the top of the steps. "Mommy!" he calls. "Mommy! I *am* like other kids." And I say, "Yes!" for he's surprised me. I say, "Yes, little boy, you are!"

child's play

*I*t is easier, we find, to make new friends in warm weather, especially when you're almost five years old and the
how of friendship is a vexing concept. Were the world the
way Jeremy would want it to be, *friend* would have a cir-
cumscribed meaning, would be applied to those rare little
boys and little girls who love the things Jeremy does with
the same overwhelming intensity. Jeremy wants a friend to
come and marvel at his toys. He wants a friend who will so
thoroughly appreciate the patterns on the floor that he is
not tempted to disrupt them. A friend is someone with
whom to compare historical or mechanical facts, exchange
one cherished piece of data for another. It's someone who
will want to sit down beside him in the middle of an afternoon and—with a held breath bespeaking utter admiration—study the pages of a textbook.

Children like that, well, they aren't a dime a dozen. So
we do the best we can, help Jeremy extend himself incre-
mentally. We begin by inviting some adults to the house.
Good friends whom we haven't seen much of for years, people we know will give Jeremy room to talk—at his speed
and at his length—about what compels him. My dear
friend Jamie comes, quietly lets herself in through the door,

and because she does not threaten to burst any invisible boundaries, Jeremy shyly sits down on the couch beside her and shows her his book about trucks. She nods when he talks about loaders, dozers, mixers, pavers, and their responsibilities in life, gives him all her attention, asks appropriate questions, waits for the response. It's a building block. It is one essential lesson out of many about how kind the world can at times be, how potentially satisfying is this thing called conversation. Paul arrives, bearing a scaled metal pickup truck and wins Jeremy's heart forever. My husband brings Patrick, an architect, home, and soon we're sitting around the table passing bread and butter, chatting like family—Patrick waiting for Jeremy to express a complicated thought before he jumps in with his own opinions. My mother and father continue to visit, new toys in hand, a perpetual eagerness to listen, and Jeremy begins running to the door when he hears them, jiggling the doorknob and welcoming them in, throwing his arms about their necks, passionately sharing a story. And then of course there's my next-door neighbor and her son, who have become, in Jeremy's mind, somewhat like family. Because they have never run forcibly through his museum of toys, because they wait for him to speak and do not hurry past him, he has let them into his heart.

Actual play with the boy next door is steadily evolving. At one time I considered the two to be at play if they were anywhere within the same house, in the same backyard, on the same playground. They were together. That was playing. That was the best that it was. But back in the fall there was a moment of marvelous synchronicity, when the neighbor and Jeremy both developed a thing for swords and knights. Jeremy preferred medieval history and my neighbor's son preferred samurai films, but for once the children

were in the same general vicinity of interest, and I capital-
ized on this every way that I could. I helped them play
upstairs in Jeremy's room—trotted each child's knights and
horses closer together until the play characters had all dis-
mounted at the same castle. I took them to the library to
read them stories about knights, encouraged them to create
little Play-Doh-style knights, got them talking to each
other about knight things, bit by bit. My neighbor and I
dressed the boys up like little knights and let them run in
circles in the yard. Whenever Jeremy got tired, I called it a
day before the experience soured.

But now the two boys are in different cycles, and though
they greet each other warmly, there's not much playing
after that—when they are together, they're in my neighbor's backyard, independently sorting through "antiques"
in a freestanding wood shed. I'm hoping that the cycles will
turn over again and that there'll be a reunion of interests,
but in the meantime it's time to move Jeremy along, introduce him to new playmates his own size.

WE TURN, OF course, to Timmy, who obviously isn't new to
Jeremy: Timmy's hosted Jeremy dozens of times, but going
to a child's house is a whole separate matter from a child
coming here. When we talk about scheduling a visit,
Jeremy grows anxious, asks in a trembling voice whether
Timmy will understand the many rules of his roadways
and cars, will know what to drive and what most definitely
must remain parked. Together Jeremy and I develop an
agenda of activities that ensures that all cars will remain
untouched—they'll build this set of Legos, they'll use these
poster paints, they'll make these stained-glass windows, I'll
read them these three books, they'll eat grapes for snacks,

they'll play cards. I walk Jeremy through what the morning will look like, remind him of what a nice boy Timmy is, and then I sit him on my lap while I make the call to Miss Janie so that nothing will surprise him about the visit.

The hour arrives. Miss Janie's big van rumbles up. Jeremy is nervously pacing the downstairs hallway. Before anyone has a chance to ring the doorbell, Jeremy grabs my hand and in a tumble of quick words asks if we can do all of our playing outside. "I'm not ready," he tells me, his face flushed, his lower lip trembling, and now the doorbell rings and I answer it alone, give Timmy a big welcome so that he will feel at home. "Isn't it a nice day?" I ask Timmy. He agrees that it is by bringing a slight pout to his mouth and a pucker of lines to his brow, and nodding once: a quick, sharp gesture. "Do you want to play some cards outside?" We have a wide, roofed porch that is hospitable to breezes, and it *is* pleasant; after all, it's early May. Playing outside would in fact be delightful.

I slip back into the house and tell Jeremy the plan. He actually says the word "Phew," takes a few deep breaths, and brushes the tears out of his luminous eyes. He walks down the hall in his floppy-laced shoes, yanks at the door (both hands on the knob), takes three more deep breaths, and greets Timmy; I walk behind him with the deck of cards in my hand. Soon Miss Janie is gone and the boys are playing. I'm playing, too, if a bit overzealously, too personally engaged. Too quick to prod the boys toward fun, I laugh with them, I admire. I know I'm reacting to the morning's nerves, and I go easy on myself about it. What we're attempting here is difficult, and we all have our own ways of coping.

By midmorning Jeremy is okay with inviting Timmy to the kitchen for a snack. After grapes and M&M cookies,

Jeremy, Timmy, and I spread out across the kitchen floor and begin moaning and groaning over a puzzle. It's got one hundred pieces. We do the smooth-sided square frame first. I keep checking the boys' faces and Jeremy seems studied and focused, until Timmy, suddenly bored, asks if he can go upstairs and play. A quick look at Jeremy tells me this would not be okay. I put the puzzle aside and pull out the stained-glass-window craft, and time runs out before anyone heads upstairs. Jeremy's nervous while the windows are baking. We have several more fresh cookies each.

The sound of Miss Janie's van scraping up the scarred driveway sends Jeremy running to the door. Timmy and I have a few private moments in the kitchen, and I bend down to his level and thank him. "Hey, Timmy," I say. "You were great today. I know Jeremy loved having you over." Timmy gives me one of his inimitable nods, collects his things like the good soldier he is, and finds his mother. Soon the van is scraping down the driveway in reverse while Jeremy sedulously waves—his fingers flat, straight, together; his forearm swinging stiffly above the fixed point of his elbow. Waving is a gesture that Jeremy's had to carefully learn, and what I'm thinking right now is how very earnest he looks, how very much like a distinguished metronome.

That afternoon I give Jeremy a little extra time alone. He held himself together throughout the morning, and I respect his need to collect himself, retreat for a while into his zone. When he's ready to talk about Timmy's visit, we quietly do—Jeremy tells me his favorite parts of the morning, talks about what frightened him, admits that he fared spectacularly well and that it would be a good thing to try it again soon. In a few weeks' time we host Timmy again, spend less time on the porch, even devote a half hour of play to the upstairs toys. An extraordinarily intelligent child with his own highly developed sense of make-believe, Timmy quickly catches on to the rules of Jeremy's road and proves himself a capable and respectful playmate. I sit in the room with my back against the wall, feigning interest in the book on my lap while in my mind, there's a single refrain: *Jeremy has two friends now. Jeremy has two friends.* Both are special kids, not run-of-the-mill, not what Jeremy will be up against in the everyday world. But it's a start, and I'm hoping Jeremy has begun to process the merits of friendship, begun to expand his definition of who and what a friend might genuinely be.

THE WARM WEATHER gives us a chance to brave more of the real world as well. Jeremy's still not ready to have just anybody over, and I'm not about to crush his emergent spirit with an ill-conceived false start. Still, the neighborhood is rich with children and homespun values, and I take Jeremy out to the street, big sticks of chalk in my fist, an idea. I draw hopscotch squares while Jeremy watches, then produce a snaking pink path studded with street signs and numbers. I start sketching caricatures of our immediate family, and because they're so lousy, Jeremy laughs.

Soon enough, some other kids have taken notice, and Jeremy and I are joined by a couple of boys, a couple of girls. Emily and Sara, Calvin, Stevie up the street, his two gorgeous sisters. They're coloring or they're hopping, they're laughing at my bad drawings, they're lithe and they're young, they're neighbors, and little by little Jeremy joins in—runs a careful distance behind the others on the dusty, smudged chalk street, straddles the curb while one of the older children ties his shoelace. The semblance of orderliness soon devolves as one game becomes several, and the sudden society grows raucous. Jeremy feels his privacy threatened, indubitably senses the potential menace of crowds, and in self-defense, he pulls away and turns around. He heads determinedly up the old misshapen marble stairs, scuttles across the cracked porch boards, opens the screen door, and vanishes. The door bangs twice before it closes. I finish a game with one of the kids, make sure everyone gets home okay, then retrace Jeremy's chalky footsteps into the house. I call him, and he comes. I take him into my arms and smile. "Did you have fun?" I ask. He nods, obedient and uncertain. "I think we did pretty well, Jeremy," I say. "I think we did." I plan for other curbside events, and Jeremy consents to attend them.

Throughout the summer, we carry out our plans. We bring toys outside and share them with the boy next door. I invite Emily and Sara for porchside stories. We acquire two drivable plastic coupes and share them with a child down the street. We bake things and distribute them on the stoop. Very few neighborhood children ever come inside; I know it's not natural, I know that it's rude, but we're not ready and I'm not going to press it. Nor do I press on Jeremy the rough-and-tumble boys, the kids you can't predict, the ones who always insist on being first. There will be plenty of time for that in life. We don't have time for it now.

moving on

*I*t is the summer of 1994, and Jeremy, newly five, doesn't have a destination for the fall. He's been attending the New Life preschool for well over a year, and though I have loved this school and am deeply indebted to its teachers for the affection and care they have given Jeremy, sending him back for another session would mean submitting him to odious redundancy: the same pair of teachers, the same exercises, the same climbing equipment, the same toys, all of it prolix except for his classmates, who, having received their fancy preschool graduation papers, have ceremoniously moved on. I have conducted a survey of the local institutional alternatives, submitted myself to the scrutiny of principals, asked questions, stacked up the facts, and now it's late July, and now it's early August, and I'm in a deep quandary over options.

There is, of course, the public school—the special-education classroom with its outstanding reputation—which seems the perfect fit for many children, but not nearly ideal for Jeremy. There are the small private schools, but interviews there are not encouraging. There are the special-education schools, few and far between, but the out-of-the-mainstream classroom wasn't right when Jeremy was three and it would be even less so now, when he has come so far, demonstrated—in a thousand telling situations—that it's the balm of ordinary life that he needs. It's my parents taking him for a drive in their new car when he needs to be wrenched out of a cycle. My neighbor inquiring after a new set of trucks when the other children are down the street, playing their games. Miss Janie serving up a sandwich at her house, then encouraging Jeremy to lounge with her sons, indulge in the make-believe of a house full of brothers. It's Jeremy's Uncle Rodi carrying him proudly on his shoulders as we meander the narrow streets of Seville, and then—another summer—up on those shoulders again, as we trek up the hills and in through the ruins of picturesque Spoleto. It's Jeremy: grandson, nephew, guy next door, most esteemed and mighty traveler. He's the king of the hill in moments like that. He is also a boy without a school.

We need to move. We need to move for a number of reasons, and we've been saying so for months, but now we've reached an impasse. There are no schools for Jeremy, and now it's September, and because I haven't done a decent job of scouting, I reluctantly return to the familiar preschool and get Jeremy settled into his room. Before the ensemble of eager, freshly scrubbed students, the teachers introduce the rules of four-year-old preschool, assign everyone a special job, and give a round of applause to the featured guest: the big letter A. *Ohh. Ahh*, the little children say. Jeremy stands and retreats to the corner, starts unstacking the tub of toys, and begins arranging last year's cars on last year's floor-tile roads. He lies all the way down and presses his cheek against the linoleum, and the only thing he moves is his hand. His eyes flicker. I know the expression. If I don't catch him now, he will soon be disappeared by cars.

Though I'm hardly necessary for navigational purposes,

I spend the morning with Jeremy at school, whispering encouragement and apologies. I make an unconvincing argument that he should sit in the circle with the assortment of new friends. He won't even look at me. Speak. No contact. Later, during recess, he climbs inside the wooden fort and sits there—moodily—and stares. "This isn't good," I say to Miss Janie. She nods. She understands that he's offended and doesn't know how to express how he feels. But for a few more weeks, we're stuck.

We need to move. I start insisting on this more emphatically now, at dinner, in the morning, when I'm taking a steaming weekend shower and my husband's on the other side of the curtain, brushing his teeth. *We need a new house in a neighborhood that has a school in which Jeremy can thrive. It's top priority. He's shutting down. We have no time to lose.* We need to move, but this isn't easy. Just having the conversation, we soon discover, is anything but easy. Generating a plan, a map for a family of three that has mastered the pacing of crisis and breakthrough while neglecting conventional foundations: baby-sitters, so that we might have time alone; boundaries, so that we might have time for the things that we love, the friends we haven't seen, the easy sleep that might renew us. It's going to be harder than we think. *Support Jeremy.* That's been our mantra. *Love him with all of our hearts.* That part's been easy. But now look at us, we're barely intelligible when it comes to giving voice to any other faction of our needs— adult companionship, a chance to dance, the prerogative to speak freely about ourselves. My husband and I don't know where we're going as husband and wife, haven't broached the subject for an eternity. We don't know where we stand as individuals or who we have separately become these past five years—me in the house, he in the city, a son between us. We don't know the ground rules, how to conduct this conversation. We don't know how to find our way. We don't expect the rush of emotions that crash in upon us when we ask, *But where should we move?*

And yet there is this issue about school. There is the point on which both my husband and I agree: Jeremy has entered a deadlock position, not just in the classroom but at home. After an uneven thaw, we feel the house refreezing—the cars getting displayed in more untouchable patterns, the insistence on long sleeves in summerish heat, the subtle constriction of Jeremy's diet until we're down to chicken, green beans, and cereal. He's pacing more and more, speaks intelligently, so passionately but exclusively of vehicles, and now he sits in the upstairs window looking down upon the train tracks that cut behind our yard, waiting for his daddy to come home. When I try to move him, he screams. When I make deals with him, he breaks them. Tells me he needs more time, he's having a thought: *Please, please, please. Mommy, don't move me. Five more minutes. Please.* We have seen these patterns before—great bits of uphill progress followed by thorny plateaus—but this time I am more frightened. I blame it on myself. Blame it on the lack of a proper school. My terrible, irresponsible planning. I should have started searching long ago. Should have gotten three steps ahead of the here and now, and conjured up an image of the future. Should have looked beneath the surface and seen that there were many questions afoot in the house, not all of them related to Jeremy. Maybe my husband wants and needs a new job. Maybe a whole other country. Maybe a wife who isn't as distracted, who can recognize the other spirits in the air.

A few weeks pass. It is my husband who concedes. Assents to a general vicinity at the other end of the train line where, I've already promised, there's an abundant crop of good schools; besides, my family is close by. As soon as I have his go-ahead, I begin to make the calls, focusing on preschools that extend through kindergarten, staying close to a script, taking no chances. We are already at a disadvantage, what with the school year already in session. I prepare a small fib for the askers: This move has come upon us suddenly; otherwise—of course—we wouldn't be asking.

We get a break at a school on a shady college campus, where the instructors by and large are students earning academic credit for their service. Only the principal is from another generation, and when I ask her, over the phone, whether the school ever takes on special needs, I get a proud and enthusiastic yes. "Right now we have a child with diabetes." I am told that I can bring my son for a four-hour morning tryout, though the principal, most likely taking a cue from my last out-of-context question, hedges her bets with a warning: "You know, we simply may find that we don't have room. And there's always the delicate issue of mix."

More confident than I have a right to be, I pack Jeremy in the car, drive fifty minutes, sustain a complicated conversation about the cars on the highway until Jeremy, at journey's end, nods off to sleep. This is the worst possible omen. No one does well when rudely jolted from sleep.

And yet Jeremy tries—valiantly—to go along with the morning routine. Sits at the computer beside another little boy, then attempts to take on the software himself. It's new to him. He fails, gets frustrated. The principal, watching from the corner of the room, strikes a check across her clipboard, and we're asked to move on and join the children in another room who are convening for a snack. There's only one slight problem with the principal's worthy plan—all but Jeremy have special, placarded chairs. When the principal asks Jeremy if he wants something to drink, he circles the room looking for space at the table, offers no answer, returns to me, hurt and teary-eyed. Another check, and we move on.

It's circle time. All the children from two to five gather in a darkened room to sing the songs they must sing every day. Adorable songs with charming hand motions and the inevitable *We all fall down*s. The kids look so darling and chipper as they wag their yellow hair. They look so normal and zesty, kindled by the possibility of a glorious soloist spot. I know some of the songs, but I've never sung them to Jeremy, and I don't believe they're staples at New Life. In the circle Jeremy sits and stares. He watches with magnificent patience and I am immensely proud, until the principal asks him if he wants to be the farmer in the dell, and pulls him to the center of the room. *What's a dell?* his eyes seem to be imploring, and what can he possibly do if he doesn't know the answer and the principal's not saying and the other children giggle until Jeremy finally sits down? Another mark on the despicable clipboard, and I throw a spear of hatred across the room.

Afterward, it is time for recess, and Jeremy, genuinely relieved, gallops all around the yard, climbs the equipment with abandon, dances to his own dervish tune—demonstrating the grace and balance he's exhibited from his start. It doesn't matter. The performance falls on dead eyes. I am ready for the principal when she approaches with her news. "I've been thinking," she tells me, with a sugary, grandmotherly smile, "that we simply don't have room. The child with diabetes is taking all our extra time, and that means we could never do right by your son."

We drive home. I curse the principal out loud, her clipboard, the damned farmer in the damned dell, and it's Jeremy who's the reasonable one, Jeremy who finally says, "I didn't like it." A well-expressed opinion for which I pull over to the roadside, climb into the backseat, and hug Jeremy until he can't breathe. His cool, incredible face against mine. His spirit that no one can impoverish. This dilemma that still presses down. I make a promise, "I will keep on trying." I drive all the way home. We read in the quiet afternoon. I take him back to New Life the next morning and he retreats into his sullen little shell.

A few more days of phone calls, and then I dial the right number. It's a chain of respected day care centers with a kindergarten program that counts, if you want it to, toward academic credit, or can also be taken as a warm-up session, a preliminary to the preliminaries of school. I'm invited in for a tour, and this time I go without my son.

Again, I meet with the principal first, a lovely girl in her mid- to late twenties who looks so young and untroubled that I'm suddenly ashamed of my appearance, terrifically self-conscious about my deplorable posture and the tenterhooks of age that are pulling at the skin around my eyes. She takes her time like a true professional and tells me about the philosophy of her school, gives me a tour of the huge center-hall house that was converted, years ago, to serve the needs of infants and toddlers. It is good to hear her talking, to be introduced to teachers, to be presented with a colorful brochure, as if I were the only one who needs to be sold on the idea of Jeremy attending this school. After an hour she inquires about Jeremy, and she asks me, as if this were an everyday question, to describe what I love most about my son.

I can barely answer. What I love most? "I guess his face," I say. "I guess his indescribable skin, how it cools me and warms me at once. His complex intelligence, his magic imagination, his mysteries, his secrets." I know I'm crying, but I continue. I know she's a stranger, but I say, "Until I had Jeremy, I didn't understand the expression 'child of God.' But now I do. I understand that God's alive in him. That my son is a spiritual presence, grander in his architecture than I will ever be."

She looks at me. I dry the skin beneath my eyes, and continue, "But there are issues. Little differences, gaps, things he might need help with, were he to come to this school. You can't be as special as he is and still fit comfortably in this world."

"Tell me more."

Groping for the right words, I slump back into my bad posture. "Well, he's not that interested in art and his fine motor skills need attention, and when you add one thing to the other, you'll probably find that he'll require extra support during crafts time."

"Okay."

"He doesn't ride a tricycle. Never seemed to want to. I've pushed him up and down the street dozens of times, but he just lets the wheels spin beneath him while he scouts for interesting cars."

"Cars?"

"Yes. His favorite thing. An obsession, some people would call it that. He has a broad and at the same time very particular understanding about cars."

"Well, he wouldn't be impressed by my car," she says, laughing kindly.

"Don't worry. He's sorely disappointed by ours."

"Okay. Fine motor concerns, gross motor delays, a car compulsion. What else?"

"I don't know if you serve your own snacks, but Jeremy's

very picky." Suddenly I'm having trouble identifying anything else that's truly troubling. I think how silly I must
look and sound, how overwrought, half sobbing in this
chair. It's me who needs the special help. Jeremy is fine.

"You can always pack what he likes, if he comes to school
here." The principal doesn't even write this snack thing
down. It's thrilling to have it fall within the bounds of normal.

I keep going, squinting to enhance my thought process.
I've gone this far, and I have to be honest, however ridiculous that honesty might sound. "Jeremy prefers to play
alone," I say. "I believe that some alone is good, but too
much of it is lonely. If he were to come, it would be so wonderful, it would actually be necessary that someone notice
just with whom and how he was playing—take some time
to acclimate him to new friends."

The principal looks at me with her untired face while
she struggles to formulate the next question. Finally she
asks it: "Is there a name for all this? A diagnosis? Or are
these just differences that we're to deal with, one at a
time?"

A name. I stall. "Well, I'm not sure the name's still valid.
If it ever was."

"That name would be . . . ?"

"Pervasive developmental disorder not otherwise specified. Actually, I think it's a catchall phrase, somewhere
between autism and normal. Jeremy is different, that's how
we tend to look at it now. He's different in a million wonderful ways, and he's also different in ways that need our
help."

The principal looks at me across the desk and tries to cal-
culate whether I'm lying. Whether I'm making things
sound better than they are so as to earn Jeremy a spot in the

school or, conversely, exaggerating so as to win over her heart. "Just a minute," she says. She stands and leaves me sitting in her office, staring out the window toward the nearby train station, miles of track from home. I can't help despising myself for blowing it again, for not giving my son a fair chance. I've said too much.

In a few minutes, the principal returns with Miss Tara, who is even younger than she is and very pretty in a wholesome way. Miss Tara has, the principal explains, experience with special needs. Carefully, accurately, the principal updates Miss Tara on all the comments I've made, and then we both wait for Miss Tara's opinion.

"I'm not precisely familiar with the sorts of issues your son seems to be presenting," she finally says. "Or, actually, I've seen the issues, but not altogether, in one child. Every little kid has his left or right of center."

"Jeremy's stumped his therapists," I tell her. "He stumped a special camp, a special school. The only thing I know for certain is that he does his best in miniature versions of ordinary classrooms, that he needs a firm hand so long as plenty of love comes along with it, and that he's losing time in the program he's in. He knows, I think, that he shouldn't be there. It's a terrific program and I adore the faculty, but he is much too old for it now. Besides, it's the same routine that he went through last year, except that all of his former classmates have moved on."

Miss Tara looks at me. I look back at her. She is at least ten years younger than me, and yet the balance of power lies entirely in her hands. I need her affirmation. I need her willingness to try. But I cannot ask for that. It's up to her.

"We have a small class," she says steadily. "We have good kids. This doesn't sound that complicated. If you work with us, we'll give it a go."

I feel another tear wend its way down my face. "I will."
I hastily blot the tear and keep my hand on my cheek, just
in case.

"We should start with a milestones list," she says. "We
can get to work on this now. What are the things you want
your son to be doing one month from today?"

"In one month?" I pause. We are moving so quickly from
uncertainty into masterminding that I have to catch my
breath. "In one month he won't be staring out the window
at the train," I offer. "He'll be trying his best at the arts and
crafts. He'll be attempting to ride the tricycle at recess. He
will look you in the eyes when you're speaking."

She writes this down. She takes my word. She doesn't get
thrown off track by this assortment of minor optimisms.

"After that I'd like to see him take some interest in the
other kids. I'd like him to remember his responsibilities,
whatever responsibilities you tend to give the kids in your
kindergarten class. And you know, really, that's all I can
think of." I've run out of steam. "I'm sure more will occur
to me over time."

"Okay," Miss Tara says. "You'll get written reports at the
end of every week. We'll talk on the phone when we need
to. If you get a brainstorm about additional milestones,
don't hesitate to call."

"Okay." The hand that's preventing the tears is wet,
warm, salty.

"So when do we get to meet your little guy?" Miss Tara
stands up and extends her hand. The principal stands.
When I stand, it feels like I am fighting a force of gravity.

"Monday. Let's start with Monday." I'm not calculating
all the hours in the car, or what it will take to really do this.
I'm not allowing for a family decision. We are taking a
place at this school. We will figure out the rest.

"We'll begin with half days," the principal tells me, smiling.

"That would be fine," I say.

"When he's comfortable, we'll increase the hours."

"Sounds like a plan." I head for the door, turn around, and say, "Thank you." There's a buzz in my ear, and I can't wait to get home, tell Jeremy the news, but impulsively, inexplicably, I take a slight detour, stop for a chocolate milk shake and a Red Delicious apple and sit in the private bubble of my car, enjoying these stolen delicacies through a silent shroud of tears.

⟵

JEREMY APPRECIATES THE adventure of his new school—loves the fact that we have to drive across turnpikes and through tollbooths to get there. He's excited in the back of the car, announces every make and model of every oncoming vehicle with gusto, reports with seriousness of manner that there are trucks threatening to overtake us in the passing lane. In the rearview mirror he occasionally finds my eyes and smiles. It's an expression that nearly throws me off the road, for when Jeremy really looks at me, really finds my center, I feel vastly connected to the whole human race, cleaned out, purified. I try to keep up with the chatter, to keep his smile on me, but mostly I feel unyoung and uncool, accumulating new driving phobias at the rate of one per mile. I'm suddenly unsure of myself on the rush-hour roadways, a little shaken by the time we get to the school, just relieved to be there, whole. Miss Tara greets us and firmly takes Jeremy's hand, and I sense, a mother's intuition, that her heart melts when she sees him. "He's a beautiful kid," she tells me over his shoulder. "I know," I say, nodding. "Exceptionally." After Miss Tara asks Jeremy a couple of

questions, after he stammers a couple of replies, the three
of us climb up the stairway, me one step behind the two of
them, Jeremy, still high and exalted from the drive, moving
heroically forward. We have to walk through a crowd of
four-year-olds before we get to the kindergarten room, and
the sight of so many makes Jeremy suddenly nervous. He
looks back at me. *Mommy?* I tell him it's all right.

There are only seven other children in the kindergarten
class, and already Miss Tara has taped Jeremy's name on
the back of a chair and a square of the table, so that he has
a place to sit. She has his name hanging from the ceiling
and his name on wall charts, a place for him on the little
helper list, a Velcro *Jeremy* that he's to place on the fuzzy
wall when he intends to use the bathroom. I want to stop
and thank Miss Tara, but I know she's only doing her job,
that she's made no exceptions here; this is how she treats
every child in this class. Jeremy runs—first thing—for the
window and the second-story view of the train tracks, and
my heart sinks until I see how Miss Tara reels him back,
collects the children for circle time, and begins the introductions. I had expected rage, fear, exorbitant shyness on
this, the first day of a new school; I had expected to stay and
ease him into the routine as I am in the practice of doing.
But Jeremy is just fine under Miss Tara's care, and I stand
in the doorway not quite knowing what to do, until Miss
Tara tells me I should come back around noon. "Let me say
good-bye to him," I tell her, and I do. He's okay with that.
A little confused, perhaps, with all the newness, but not
feeling frightened or forsaken. I descend the wide stairs;
the principal is waiting at the landing. "Everything seems
to be going quite well," I tell her. I don't say anything else
for fear of crying again, so I mumble, "See you at noon,"
and I open and shut the front door. It's October. The trees

are brilliant. I stand on the front stoop and blink at the sun.

Two months from now, we will buy a tiny Tudor house no more than a mile from this school. We will pack our entire life into boxes, forcibly dislodging the established patterns, discarding that which is no longer useful, salubrious, or desirable. We will say good-bye to the neighbors whom we almost got to know, run the vacuum over the carpet one last time for the childless couple who will fill out our house, unshutter the windows, send the remains of us flying, perhaps weed the garden patch along the one side that I never seemed to get to. We will break bad habits in the new house of ours. Learn the meter of shared dreams; keep the doors open, at least partway; read the notes Miss Tara sends. All of this will come to us, we have earned it as a family, but for now, it is me on these steps alone and Jeremy upstairs at school, both of us headed off in the right direction.

the farmer in the dell

*T*he new house is in fact quite old, requires massive renovation. Of its six total rooms, only three are genuinely inhabitable, and of these three, two are set aside as storage bins, holding tanks for every box and stick of furniture the movers dredge out of their whiz-bang truck. That leaves us the long, white-stucco family room with its colossal, curtainless windows, and this is where we squeeze our beds, our dressers, our books, a single carton of favorite miniature cars. This leaves us as well with the construction crew—a carpenter, a painter—that has promised to produce a modest upstairs before Christmas. It's early December. We're spending every spare penny. This house is our gift to us. At night, after the crew goes home, we lie together in our makeshift bedroom while the moon passes over our heads. The nights are the color of lapis lazuli. Jeremy stays awake as long as he can, and his eyes look like two bursts of light.

During the day, there is hardly any room to lay out the cars—we're packed in that tight—but Jeremy's spending most of his time at school and growing stronger, more self-confident every moment. He is performing the most essential acts—following the classroom routine, running errands between his second-floor classroom and the principal's office downstairs, even helping out with the younger children on Special Helper Day. There are issues, certainly—a habit of crayoning outside the lines on the work sheets (faint scratches of color and he's done), still no curiosity about bats, balls, or bikes, a decided preference for individual problem-solving initiatives over group activities—but Miss Tara and I agree not to sweat the small stuff. The milestones have been surpassed: Jeremy has adjusted, is not lying on the floor at an insurmountable distance, is trustworthy with tasks, is greeted warmly by his classmates. I see this when I dally in the morning during drop-off or when, in the afternoon, I arrive a quarter of an hour early and watch the playground from afar. I make it clear to Miss Tara that she is in charge, that I trust her to steer Jeremy's course through school, turning the pressure on and off as she sees fit. Meanwhile, I am bursting with pride, full of respect for this child who has already mastered the hardest things in life and is teaching them, by example, to me. For instance: perseverance. For another instance: the unbounded largesse of the heart. More and more, Jeremy is becoming the thing that I turn to, the spirit I gather in my arms when I need to be tranquil and windless, need straightening out, get caught in Lilliputian details and want to be joggled back to life. Just sitting with Jeremy realigns my priorities. I look at him and I know what's important, can dismiss the frustration of a freelance writing project or the insensitivity of a client on the line.

BUT BY JANUARY it is time—again—to make a determination about Jeremy's future. He has been under Miss Tara's care for only four months now. He's doing extraordinarily well. We are hopeful.

There are a number of decisions we have to make. Private school or public school. Therapeutic interventions, no interventions. First grade or kindergarten. How far am I willing to drive? After a few preliminary conversations with school administrators, it's clear that we're not going anywhere without more tests, more recent documentation regarding Jeremy's standing in relation to the world's great norms. We make arrangements with one of the most-respected professionals in town, and we provide her with all the paperwork she asks for. Even Miss Tara contributes to the official record, writing a note that, in part, says this: *Jeremy is always listening but does not need to make eye contact in order to do so. He's very talkative with people he is formally introduced to. Not unlike other children, Jeremy needs a break from work and needs positive reminders about how to perform certain skills such as fine and gross motor. He performs all of his academic skills successfully when he feels comfortable and safe about his surroundings. Jeremy is a pleasure to have in the class and is always learning new things.*

In early February, during a three-hour session, Jeremy undergoes a battery of tests: the Stanford-Binet Intelligence Scale: Fourth Edition; the Wechsler Preschool and Primary Scale of Intelligence; the Peabody Picture Vocabulary Test, Form L; the Boston Naming Test; the Achenbach Child Behavior Checklists; the Vineland Adaptive Behavior Scales; the Thematic Apperception Test, Selected Cards; the Children's Apperception Test Supplement; Kinetic Family Drawing; Sentence Completion Form—Young Children. I sit in the lobby, nervous and unsettled, making excuses for a weak performance. Too much at once in an unfamiliar setting. Shutdown in the company of strangers. He didn't eat enough for breakfast. He's either too cold or too hot. I have a V. S. Naipaul book on my lap, and over the entire three hours I don't manage to turn a page.

At noon, Jeremy's delighted and happy, pleased as punch with himself. I can hear him clopping down the hallway, chattering freely. I see him: all smiles on his stunning face. The doctor turns the corner into the reception room a few steps after Jeremy, and my heart is pounding: *How did he do?*

"He's wonderful," she tells me. "And he did quite well. Better on some things than on others, of course. Give us a few days to tabulate the results."

"You're the best." I sweep Jeremy into my arms. "You're amazing. I love you so much."

"Can I have some juice?" Jeremy asks. I present the juice box that's been waiting; then, after the doctor is gone, I sneak him a wedge of milk chocolate.

➤

I'M HAPPY, FEARFUL, noisy as I wait for the results. On the day of the parent conference, I can't stop pacing. When my husband and I finally take our chairs in the physician's office, I feel my heart flopping around in my chest. I have to lean in toward the doctor so that I can hear what she says. Otherwise, her words would drown in my anxious jumble.

Jeremy is, she begins, a lovely child who has clearly made great progress over the last three years. He has some superior skills (memory) and some right-on-par ones; he attends to his tasks in a methodical, unhurried fashion, asking for help when he feels that he needs it rather than getting trapped in a cycle of frustration. There are also areas where Jeremy still needs to catch up—learning to tell a story from beginning to end, for example, or mastering irregular plurals; tying his shoelaces; wiping his nose when he sneezes;

blowing out candles and brushing his teeth; apologizing for social faux pas; using scissors; catching a ball; hopping on one foot without losing balance; coloring within the lines; understanding the basic safety issues. Of greatest concern is his loneliness. While he speaks of wanting friends, it's clear that he'd prefer to play alone with his rules than collaboratively compromise.

"On the basis of the current assessment, it is clear that Jeremy's knowledge of word meanings, as well as the ability to express those meanings, and his word-retrieval skills are well above the strict average for his age," she continues. "At the same time, it is felt that Jeremy remains somewhat vulnerable in both the interpersonal realm and in the area of language development. At this point he needs support to build on his social skills, including his skills in the social or pragmatic use of language."

It's an incredibly accurate and thorough report; we believe she has seen our son for all he is, created an environment in which he felt safe enough to be able to perform at full potential. We thank the doctor profusely for her commitment, her energy, her time. We talk awhile about our schooling options, but in the end she says it's up to us: send him to first grade with a phalanx of tutors and special aids, or wait a year, grow his confidence in a private kindergarten setting, where the classrooms are small and forgiving and he can begin to work on his small social being.

We don't struggle very much with the decision. It's time to treat the interaction issues. We'll supplement the academic component at home, and we'll bring more conviction to sharpening some of those everyday skills—blowing one's nose, brushing one's own teeth, accepting some household responsibilities—that we've been letting slide to date. First grade would demand too much of Jeremy on all fronts, we believe. Another year of kindergarten would be a much kinder entry to school life. As much as I would love to see Jeremy return to Miss Tara's care next year, we both know the redundancy would be stifling, and so I spend conference time with Miss Tara alone, while she lays out what she perceives to be the ideal classroom setting.

After a round of phone calls, I narrow my sights on two schools, both of them in the Quaker Friends tradition, one out west in the country, one more urban in aspect. I like the philosophy of the Friends schools, their celebration of diversity, the way the children are taught to teach one another. I like the idea of Jeremy working in a miniature version of the mainstream, observing everyday children at play, modeling his behavior on theirs. I know for a fact that Jeremy needs small classrooms, kindness, protection, support. I know that he doesn't grow unless he feels safe. The director of admissions at the Quaker school in the country spends a lot of time answering my questions, sharing some of her own story, for she is a mother herself, of two sons. I grow to trust her. I value her insights. I begin to believe that there aren't two choices; rather, there is one: Jeremy will become a country Quaker.

Of course, my opinion is just my opinion. The decision lies in other hands. Every private school has its tryout tradition, and the country Quakers are no different. On a very cold day in the middle of winter, we dress Jeremy in new clothes and scrounge around for a stuffed brown bear. Bringing the bear with us is one of the tryout conditions, and I'm a little nervous about this: if Jeremy's affection for furry stuffed animals is on trial, this is a case we're going to lose. Only one furry friend has ever captured his imagination, and that's the dinosaur he sleeps on, like a pillow.

But we bring the bear. We help Jeremy manage some pre-tryout jitters, then we wait, with other parents, in the small school library. Within one hour, the children are returned to us, more or less beaming beneath piles of construction-paper projects. They have drawn pictures of their families, cut and pasted the parts of teddy bears, sung songs, we're told, shared stories. As the last one back to the reception room, Jeremy is chaperoned by the head kindergarten teacher, who has her arm placed gently across his shoulder. "You have a beautiful kid," she tells us, looking at him longer than she really needs to. "We really enjoyed having Jeremy today."

"Thank you," we say. "We enjoyed being here."

"Okay," she smiles, shakes our hands firmly. "Well." I know Jeremy's struck a chord in this teacher's heart. Ridiculously sure that Jeremy's broken the code, that we have a place on this ramshackle campus, in her classroom.

We drive home and I'm extra cheery, high on adrenaline, imagining myself friends with other mothers at that school, imagining Jeremy as one of the gang. "It's all settled," I tell my husband. "Don't you think?" I hold Jeremy's construction-paper evidence in my hand—his stick picture of the three of us, his cut-and-paste teddy bear project in which, I think, Jeremy's shown his budding sense of humor. Instead of pasting the circles in positions suggesting head, belly, arms, and legs, Jeremy's taken his circles and stacked them, one on top of the other, so that what he has is a telescoping swirl of blue. "He must have thought the teddy bear project was stupid," I say, laughing to my husband. Then, over my shoulder, "Didn't think much of the blue bear, did you?"

"Nope," Jeremy answers, after he processes the question. "I hate . . . I hate . . . I hate teddy bears."

"You get that from me," I tell him. "It's genetic."

⟶

I WAIT THAT week for a call of confirmation, move some cash around in the bank so as to have the deposit moneys at the ready. I'm waiting in vain. We don't hear back from the director of admissions for several weeks, and when I finally call, faking nonchalance on my end, there's hesitation, an indication that there may not in fact be enough spaces in the kindergarten class. I'm encouraged to look elsewhere just in case things don't work out well, and I do not have the wherewithal to prod around for reasons: it's as if someone had taken excellent aim and socked the wind out of my solar plexus. I'm stumbling around in the house, trying not to let Jeremy in on the disappointment I feel.

I'm also back on the phone, arranging an appointment at the second Quaker facility, where I'm assured that there's room aplenty, that the teachers would love to meet my son, that the administrators will even work around our schedule, but my heart's not in the interview, the tour. No doubt about it, the new facility is a gorgeous construction, replete with an upscale cafeteria, state-of-the-art playground structures, an impressively equipped gymnasium. Everything looks perfect, and yet I start looking around for cracks in the ceiling, stubby crayons, a kid playing alone in a corner, a painting in the hallway gallery that stands out from the crowd, anything to suggest that a boy with differences could fit in. I don't see these things, and this concerns me. I know enough about Jeremy now to recognize that this wonderful place would prove intimidating, could lead to withdrawal.

Jeremy needs a place that he can gradually work himself
into, a school that will accept a divergent journey toward
general goals. Although it's only intuition, my heart tells
me this place isn't right. It's right for so many other families, but it isn't right for ours, and when you are choosing a
school, you can't accept compromise. You can't tempt fate
by plunking the child down in the wrong place.

Determined not to let my son down, I drive home and
dial the number of the school in the country, wait for the
director of admissions to come on, and, without much of an
introduction, retrace the developmental history of my son.
I talk about the echolalia, the pronomial reversals, the
haunting social phobias he's conquered; talk about his successful, odds-beating assimilation into ordinary schools.
Talk about his character, his integrity, his incredible loving
gestures, his feats of memory, his passions, his seductive
eyes, his potential, his courage. Quote Miss Tara. Quote the
recent test scores. Say, emphatically, that Jeremy's a con-
tributor, that he would make a contribution to that class.
And besides, I love the school, and I really can't imagine
taking Jeremy anywhere else. Is there anything I can do?
Any other questions I can answer? Any guarantees I can
offer?

The director of admissions listens for a long time, then
says it's genuinely a matter of space. There's much more
interest in the class than they can actually accommodate,
and they're waiting for a few undecideds to sort themselves
out.

"Is Jeremy at the *bottom* of the list?" I ask baldly.

"He did have some performance issues," the director
admits. "Didn't do quite as well as the other children.
Although we loved him. We all did. We can see tremendous
potential."

"Like what?" I ask, my voice suddenly timid. "Like what performance issues?" This is something I didn't expect. She has more facts than I do.

"There were eye-contact problems, slowness of speech, nerves in the classroom, an inability to follow the directions with the cutout teddy bear."

"But he hates teddy bears," I say. "Hates them. So do I. Don't you? I mean, *God*. I mean, if you had asked for a project that involved planes or cars, he would certainly have emerged as your star student."

"How much are you willing to work with us on this?" the director asks, after a few moments.

"I'm willing."

"Honestly? We're still facing the issue of space. It's tight this year. But we're interested in your son and we'll keep in touch. We just need to wait and see."

A FEW WEEKS later, we get the good news: they have found room for Jeremy at the country school. We are ecstatic, believe strongly that Jeremy will be going to the right place next year—a small classroom, no pretension, loving teachers, a school that emphasizes collaborative play and shared learning. Under Miss Tara's expert care, we finish out the current year, experience our highs and lows. We get stuck in places, we move on. Jeremy starts to come home speaking of a little boy named Mikey. I ask Miss Tara, and she confirms that the two are friendly. Not quite ready to start visiting each other's homes, but definitely there's the start of a friendship there, a budding mutual-admiration society.

On the last day of school, Miss Tara's small class comes together beneath the heat and chill of a setting sun. All the parents are there in the white-picket-fence school yard, waiting for the ceremony to begin. I stand with my husband right up front, a perfect view of the procession that begins to spin out of the building, down a ramp, into the yard. Jeremy brings up the rear with his handmade cap on. He's a graduate. He did it. He's feeling proud.

After the calling of names and the distribution of gifts and diplomas, a family picnic for which I've neglected to bring blankets, Miss Tara and her cohorts lead the families and kids in song. We all sit in a circle on the damp grass and wait for the singing to begin, my husband at my side, Jeremy half on his lap, half on mine. When it does, when "If I Had a Hammer" starts rising up, toward the evening, Jeremy knows all the words, and even sings them. Sings "Bingo," sings about Mary's lamb, even sings that damned "Farmer in the Dell." It's not typically a tearjerker, but I'm sitting here wet-eyed. If only they—every doubting they— could see us now.

wings

*T*onight we are somewhere above the sea in the infinity of night. We have been flying for several hours now, and most passengers are asleep. The cabin is dark but for the strip of theater-like floor lights and the hot dots of the individual lamps of insomniacs. My husband and son have their own lights switched on, and out of the corner of my eye I watch their peaceful goings-on. They both have their trays down. They're both hunched eagerly forward. There's a piece of paper on Jeremy's tray and a piece of paper on my husband's, and both of them are drawing.

It's an interest Jeremy has just lately grabbed onto. He still colors his own way and paints passively, his eyes roving away from the brush, but drawing is a skill he wants to master. "Daddy," he'll say, "draw me an F-14 Tomcat," and my husband, with the artistry that won me over in the first place, has always pushed everything else aside and produced a perfect Tomcat on the page. Or the menu. Or the napkin. Or the little notepad he has begun to carry about, just to support spontaneous notions such as these. My husband has sketched, and Jeremy has watched, and then Jeremy has bitten his lip and gripped his marker and furiously produced his own Tomcat. Jeremy's Tomcats don't always look precisely like Daddy's, and he's shed a few tears about that. But that doesn't stop him from trying again, or from listening, carefully, as my husband explains that every object on earth is built out of everyday shapes, and the trick lies in recognizing the angles. The circles. The squares.

A favorite pastime, the last few weeks, has been a stepsister of drawing: line mazes. First Jeremy got fascinated with the ones we found in books, an accidental discovery. I bought every last workbook I could find on the subject, then sat and applauded while he drew his way from point A to point B. Given Jeremy's extraordinary memory, there was no repeating a maze puzzle once solved, and he was beginning to feel plundered by the lack of new challenges when my husband started drawing originals. Wonderful little road webs with all manner of streetside attractions and carefully printed instructions that Jeremy instantly adored. "Make me a maze," is the first thing Jeremy now tells his father whenever he hears him come through the door. Daddy never fails to comply.

Now Jeremy himself has become a maze maker. Every afternoon upon returning from summer camp, he clears a spot at his battered worktable and announces, "I'm making Daddy a project." He draws a line at the top, workbookstyle, where my husband is to print his name, then he strains and he stutters over a multibranching roadway, a dozen arteries emanating from a central hub, all of them blocked at some point but for one. "Ooeeoh, this is a tough one," he'll warn me again and again. "Daddy's never going to get this right." I'll say, "Hey, can you make a maze for me, too?" and Jeremy says, with all the genuine sweetness in the world, "Of course not. My mazes are for Daddy." I don't really blame him. My talent is not rooted in mazes. Still, it would be nice to be included.

In this plane tonight, Jeremy and his daddy have drawn what in our house is called World War III fighter planes—which is any aircraft built after World War II. They have drawn a car or two. They haven't drawn people—Jeremy has no interest in that—and now they're hunched over separate mazes that they'll trade in a few moments, for each other's review. I have only one eye on them. Occasionally I look out the window. It's pitch-black up here above the weather. We're making little progress against the moon.

When I fly I think about all the spirits we're passing through. The few I knew and the billions I didn't, their vapors mingling in the air all around us. My grandmother is up here somewhere, pinning a hat to her head; my favorite uncle decorating the universal Christmas tree; my father's parents; my great-aunts and -uncles; children I have heard about on the news; great writers. I think of them when I'm aloft in an airplane. I think of the extreme significance of every single human being and the vast insignificance of us all. The earth is just one rock in a universe without limits; we exist in the blink of an eye. We are impossibly small against this dimensional hugeness, and yet we care, gigantically, about our place in things, survival. We attend to the tiny details of our lives, attend to one another, make room for the miracle of a child. Put his toys in a bag and draw him mazes and take him to places, for adventure. Fight the systems and labels on his behalf so that he, in turn, can fight the systems for others.

I carried Jeremy inside me for nine complete months, then labored for thirty-six hours. I think about this now because today is Jeremy's birthday; on my watch we

approach the birthing hour. During the first pangs of dis-
comfort, I was impressively upright—even ran down the
street after a long-overdue truck. *That's my kid's furniture,*
I screamed, all the way down the block. *Turn around! Turn
around! You've got my kid's crib.* A few hours later, I was
curled, throbbing and miserable, on the couch, trying to
finish one last issue of a newsletter whose audience cared
deeply about money. After that, I was pacing our ugly-car-
pet hallway, clutching and clawing at my back. I called the
doctor at hysterical intervals. He assured me that I should
try to get some sleep. My husband expressed the exact same
opinion, even offered a real-life demonstration, but sleep
had become an abstract concept for me; I waited anxiously
for dawn. At the first sign of sun, I called my mother,
grabbed my suitcase, trundled heavily into the car. Two
hours later, I was in full-fledged labor in a much-overused
speckled gown. My husband, well rested, was standing
guard by the machines. The doctor, not as well rested, was
smiling falsely. Out in the hospital lobby, my parents were
waiting; so were Jane and J.C., two friends who'd gotten
news of the event. From 10:00 in the morning to 11:30 that
night, I endured the common rituals of childbirthing,
obsessed over the comfort of my lobby guests, screamed in
every language at the doctor, wondered if my guests could
hear me screaming. At 11:49, in the sudden vacuum of
white silence, Jeremy made his way into the world. He's
been glowing starlike ever since. Someday he'll join the
vapors of the night, help my uncle trim that tree.

"Happy sixth birthday, Jeremy," I whisper, reaching for
him. "Yeah," he says, "yeah," never lifting his eyes from his
mazes. I wait eleven minutes, then kiss my husband on the
cheek. "And happy birthday to you," I tell him. Because
that's how it is. Their birthdays, like everything else about

them, are conjoined in space and time. They take the same step forward every year, at the same time. They face the vastness together. They teach each other the particulars of progress. They fly forward and forward, on their uncommon wings.

quaker friends

*W*eather permitting, he walks the mile to school—a tall, big-booted man whose beard falls from his chin like crinoline. He wears a cap and a lumberjack's shirt, and as he treks through the stubble of the Quaker graveyard, he fiddles in his trouser pocket for a key, tracing its metal teeth with his thumb while he considers the tasks of the day. At the door he crouches slightly, attends to the lock, pulls at the brass doorknob, and lets himself in—displacing the stoppered night air with the smells of the farm from which he's come, the smells of the morning, spilled milk, freshly cut grass. With snaps of light, he fills the upper schoolhouse rooms—the first room, the second room, the third room, the hallway—stirring things up, shuffling the papers in their bins, rescuing a fallen Pilgrim with a fresh doughnut of tape. An hour or so and the teachers will come. After that: the children with their swollen lunch bags, their friendships, their fears, the hats, scarves, mittens that they will inevitably lose and he most certainly find—later, on the other side of this day. The mothers will call him names for the things he does—Our Guardian Angel—but the man goes by Saunders, simple enough, and it seems to me that he'd like to keep it that way, like to garner no attention for his kindness.

I don't know Saunders the way I should know Saunders. I cannot describe his job except to say that he loves the scattered, misfit buildings of the country day school that employs him, loves the meetinghouse, the distant grange, the sorrel trailer. He loves the antique hill at the modern intersection: the green and granite, the gate, the dusty soccer bowl, the fort house, the swing set, the marble inscriptions to the graveyard dead, the cumbersome collection of old trees. Saunders loves this place, and he's its watchman—throwing blankets on its roofs in nasty weather, plugging holes in plaster walls, dismantling a squirrel's trove of leaking walnuts, piecing remnants of carpet into patterns on the floor. He dusts the steps with salt in winter. Scoops the fallen leaves out of the gutters. Mows the grass with a miniature tractor. Balances a time-wrecked table with a freshly carved wooden leg. The tools fit easily into Saunders' oversized hands. His job has a sound to it, a music.

A bachelor, Saunders lives on a corner parcel of his father's farmland in a house I imagine he constructed himself, though I don't know that for sure. Thanksgivings, he once told me, are spent splitting wood, following a breakfast of pork butts with his father. Summers are spent imagining the farmer he might have been, had his old man not sold half the fertile acreage to a conniving land developer. Nights Saunders spends tooling around with his checkerboard pickup, scratching mottoes into its wide tailgate, little pearls he's fished out of his head. In the morning, Saunders laces his boots and starts on the brief jaunt to school, while the sun breaks over the edge of the planet.

JEREMY DID NOT take easily to his first few months of kindergarten at the country school upon the hill. The first days, the first several weeks, he was beset by mysterious stomach ails, gripping pains beneath the rib cage that subsided, strangely enough, the instant he was safely belted back inside the car. He spent September with his head on the kindergarten classroom's rickety tables, tears in his eyes, classmates tapping his shoulder: *Are you all right? Do you want to see what I made?* The crayons fell from his hands to the floor. Circle time induced a panic. Recess was entirely unmanageable for him; he ran in circles to avoid the other children.

Jeremy's tears incited sympathy at first, but by the end of the first few weeks I found them to be alarming. His teachers were concerned, as were the principal and the other children, and it was clear without anybody saying so that we had broken the first promise of our engagement: Jeremy was not adjusting to Quaker friendship, and his anxiety was a serious problem. In my eyes, in fact, it was becoming dangerous, for with the school year now in full swing, there were not a lot of options for Jeremy. The high-tuition special schools had long since been filled to capacity. The public school, with its many children and impatient directives, would, I knew, erode the important ground he'd bravely covered. For another mother, home schooling might have been a feasible alternative, but the education Jeremy most needed now involved instructions on conversability, amiability, and play—lessons I was ill equipped to deliver.

Every morning, during our lengthy drives to the school, Jeremy and I would have a little conversation. My tactics changed as the days disappeared, and as I grew increasingly carking. "Don't be afraid of kindergarten," I advised him at first, silencing another voice in my head that wanted to

warn him, *Be careful.* "Your school's such a terrific place—
those hand-sewn puppets, those gingersnaps. I envy you.
Wish I could go. You lucky kid, going to school."

A few days later, I offered a different sort of palliative,
telling Jeremy I could imagine how he felt, knew what he
was going through, trusted completely that in time he'd settle down. "That old stomach of yours is just being silly," I
whispered conspiratorially. "It's playing some mean tricks
on you." When that didn't work, I started in with questions:
"What's your favorite part of school?" "Who do you like to
sit with in the morning?" "Can you teach me how to count
to ten in the Spanish I know you're learning?"

I wasn't helping. Jeremy's eyes were red at pickup time,
and when I'd ask the teacher if she'd seen any improve-
ments, she'd shake her head and say tomorrow would be
better. Now in the car I began pressing harder for information, for compliance; I made small threats. "Is there something I don't know, Jeremy? Something that feels strange,
something you want to talk about. . . . I'm listening . . . I'm
waiting . . . I'm listening." Granted no answer, I persisted:
"Are you sure you have a stomachache, Jeremy? Are you
sure that's why you're crying? If it's a stomachache, Jeremy,
then I guess we'll see a doctor. You tell him where it hurts.
You tell him why."

A few weeks of my own uninterrupted monologue, a few
weeks of no progress, a few too many sleepless nights, and
I resorted to flat-out truth-telling: "You need to help yourself, Jeremy," I asserted emphatically. "You need to do a
good job. We've been given a chance here, one chance, and
if this school doesn't work out, if they say we don't belong,
then I don't know what we'll do. I don't know if there's
another place on earth for us, Jeremy, and I'm afraid to find
that out."

At home I avoided the phone for fear of hearing an entreaty. I expected the sound of the principal's voice, or the teacher's. I expected another mother to call and complain about the disruptions caused by my son, but miraculously those phone calls never came. The Quakers were giving us time, and their time is what we needed—their faith, their friendship, their suspended verdict, and a man named Saunders, in casual jeans and a hay-colored beard, a man who fixed school things for a living because his father had sold off half the farm.

JEREMY'S FRIENDSHIP WITH Saunders had impalpable origins; I'm not sure anyone could say how it began. Maybe Saunders heard the cries of the kindergarten boy and recognized a kindred sadness in the heart. Maybe, tapping a nail into the classroom easel or straightening a new shelf of books, Saunders noticed the dark-haired child slowly taking solace in a shoe box of bright cars and remembered a childhood fancy of his own. Maybe Saunders respected the gentleness of the one who cried too much, saw that he would never hurt another, saw that he was trying, hard, to arrest his emotions by taking deep, gasping swallows of air. Maybe Saunders was just being Saunders, taking care of broken objects at the school.

That September and October, as far as I could tell, Saunders went about his chores as usual—polishing the benches in the meetinghouse, sanding the splinters from the playground structures, pulling down felt boards, taping the bookworms up high on the walls. He came to school in the morning and he went home after dark, and though I saw him often enough, exchanged casual hellos, sometimes wondered about his life beyond the antique hill, my mind was on Jeremy and the classroom, on the question: *Will my son finally acclimate himself to school?*

By early November, there were signs that things were changing. Jeremy's eyes were calmer when I came to pick him up, and his teacher had some stories she could tell. Good stories. "Jeremy participated in today's craft," I was told one afternoon. "It was hard for him, but he stuck with it, took the project all the way through." A few days later: "Jeremy raised his hand at circle time today. He answered the question that I asked; he didn't get flustered." One night, even, I received a telephone call. It being late, I expected the worst. "Jeremy's making progress," his teacher reported, over the line. "Today he played, for a few minutes, with another child." In the heart of that night, I made no attempt to mask my feelings. The teacher, miles away, didn't mask hers, either.

With Jeremy clearly edging forward, I pulled back whenever I could. Stopped asking the grating questions in the car. Didn't search for stories, explanations, didn't go where it didn't make sense to go. If Jeremy was happy, then so was I. If he was gradually finding his fit in that school, I knew enough to get out of the way, to give Jeremy time alone with his thoughts after he was back in the car with me. Later, I would teach him about dangers and precautions. For now, he had to blaze his own small trails.

⌒

I should explain that I had started to leave Jeremy for longer hours at the school; following kindergarten's dismissal near noon, he stayed for an after-school program of structured crafts, games, and song. More exposure to other kids was the best thing for him, and the woman who ran the program had good ideas—was perpetually recycling milk cartons, pipe cleaners, paper towels, plastic spoons into examples of exceptional art. Sometimes, I suppose, she needed Saunders' handy skills—must have called him in off his tractor or down from the roof when the stapler was jammed or the box of Lincoln logs wouldn't open. Perhaps, after a while, Saunders simply arranged his task list differently—did all the outside things in the morning during true school hours, stayed close to the program in the afternoon. I can't imagine Saunders insisting on this himself, but I do believe that he was there when he was needed, and need, Saunders clearly understood, didn't always pertain to jammed playthings. Need also pertained to the six-year-old boy who could be easily undone by small society.

It seems, therefore, that Saunders occasionally helped Jeremy with his confounding coat zipper or hat. Reached for a box of toys high on the shelf. Retrieved a truant car from beneath the table. Jeremy never said so, but something like trust must have grown between them, and one day when I came to the school on the hill to take Jeremy home, it was just the two of them in the classroom, the others having gone elsewhere to play. I heard them before I saw them—the plucking sounds of an old banjo; Jeremy singing, unselfconsciously, to "O, Susanna." When I reached the doorway, I stood there unnoticed and watched, amazed, as Saunders, perched upon a tabletop, played, and Jeremy danced jauntily before him. Both seemed lost, a little, in the song—Saunders in his banjo, Jeremy in his fearlessness—and it wasn't so much a performance they were sharing as it was an open moment in time. A friendship, while I watched like an intruder from the door.

FOR CHRISTMAS THIS year, we want everything special. Jeremy and I spend considerable time looking for the right gifts for the people in his school: the teachers, the principal, the woman at the front desk, and Saunders, for whom, after much discussion, we settle on a museum-quality mug. Together, happily, we wrap the presents, and on the day preceding the holiday break, we drive our ribboned presents to the school. Jeremy makes the special deliveries while I wave, from a distance, behind, and I am so caught up in the sociability of things that I don't notice Saunders approaching. "Ma'am?" he says, when he is already quite close. "I have a little something for Jeremy."

"You do?" I step back. "A gift for Jeremy?" The possibility had never occurred to me; I'm not confident that I heard what he said.

"Yes, well. Something I made," he answers shyly. "Just a little something I put together in the shop." Saunders reaches into his pocket now and does not retrieve a key. He retrieves a hand-carved jeep instead—a wooden four-wheel drive that fits in the palm of his hand.

"You made this?" I ask him. Jeremy has turned the corner, is presenting a gift. He's not here yet; I'm the only one who sees this.

"Yes. Well. In the shop." He seems apologetic, though that's not possible. The little jeep is smooth as butter and full of a craftsman's details—a curved windshield, four rugged tires, a big spare tire on its back.

"Saunders," I say, genuinely moved. "It's such a treasure. Jeremy will love it. Really. You've been so kind."

"Just a little something," Saunders assures me. "Your son's a real good kid."

"I don't know how to thank you, Saunders," I tell him, truthfully. "Not just for this. For everything. For the songs

you've played on the banjo, and for I don't know what else."
The jeep is in my hand now. Jeremy is still just out of sight.
I can see the trace of a smile in Saunders' beard.

"Don't mind a bit, ma'am," Saunders answers. "Really.
Jeremy's good to me, too. We're sort of friends."

"He's feeling more at home here, Saunders. Don't you
think?" I ask him hopefully.

"Yes, ma'am," Saunders concludes. "I reckon he is.
Sometimes the important things just end up taking time."

a slant of sun

*C*aught in a stray slant of sun at the head of the table, Jeremy is all spoon and squint. A bowl sits before him, and a corn- and wheat-colored box. "Hunn-*ee*," he reports, turning his filled-to-capacity spoon upside down to scratch his ear. "Bun-*chess*. Mommy?" he finally reaches across the table, taps me on my shoulder, and asks, "What does Hunn-*ee* Bun-*chess* of Oahts mean?"

"You're eating it," I answer him casually enough, though the question thrills me. "Look in your bowl."

"Oh," Jeremy replies thoughtfully, casting his dark eyes toward the hardwood table, the chipped white-and-blue dish, the puddles of saturated flakes that have fallen unlikely distances from their starting place. A dribble of milk turns the corner of his chin. His helter-skelter spoon remains suspended in midair. "Hunn-*ee* Bun-*chess*," he repeats. "That means cereal."

"Only the kind you're eating right now," I attempt a clarification. "Other cereals have other names." Jeremy's hair looks like cinnamon in the shaft of sun. Whatever he is thinking has changed the patterns of his face, the arches in his eyebrows, his lips.

"Oh," Jeremy says, after a long pause. "So. The words on the box explain the thing that's inside."

"You've got it." Close to applause, I avoid the blunder. "Most boxes most of the time explain what's inside them with words," I continue, like an academic. I try to think of an exception so that the world of boxes, advertisements, displays will never play a trick on my son, won't prove me wrong, but my mind goes blank. Though I've long since finished my breakfast and should be packing Jeremy's things for school, though I know I'll have to drive too fast if he's to appear in class on time, I wait: a perpetual rebel for his cause.

"So," Jeremy says, digging his spoon back into his bowl as if he has all day, no prior appointments. "Words on boxes are for explaining. Words in books are for stories. Words on traffic signs are so you don't get crashed." Triumphant, he brings the spoon toward his face, but given the instrument's awkward angle, he's greeted with the tongue-burning taste of cold metal. It doesn't bother him; he tries again. Same angle, same result, until I lean across the table and gently adjust the flatware in his hand. "I can't read everything," Jeremy tells me. "But some things I can."

"You're an *amazing* reader," I sing at him, from my heart. "Who taught you how?" I succumb to teasing so that what I'm feeling will not show. Since I've been asking the same question for many consecutive months, Jeremy reads the joke out of my words and answers, predictably, "*I* did."

"*You* taught yourself to read?" I ask, feigning surprise.

The predictable delay, the response: "Yup."

"Just figured it out one day?"

"Yup."

"Well then, you're a very smart little boy." I push my chair back to stand, then bow toward Jeremy and rinse my fingers through the spice colors of his hair. "You're also handsome," I whisper. "Do you know what that means?"

"That I'm smart?" Jeremy asks me, eager to be right.

"You're handsome *and* smart," I say. "Both things at once. It can be done," I assure him. "However rarely."

"I can't read everything," Jeremy warns me again. "I'm just a kid." His unalloyed honesty brings me down into my seat again, and I know that it's impossible now. We'll never get to school on time.

"Hey, I can't read everything, either," I confide quietly to Jeremy, leaning close to him, tracing the rim of his ear. "At my age, I should be able to, but I can't." Jeremy is making soup out of his cereal now, harmlessly banging his useless utensil against the interior lip of the bowl, looking at anything but me.

"What can't you read?" he asks out of nowhere, not looking up. It's a stunning question. An inquiry about me, my life. I have to regulate my breathing before I can reasonably respond.

"Oh my, Jeremy," I respond, flustered. I want to get this answer right; it's so important. I want it to be worth his while to hear the story he's invited. "I can't read anything if it isn't in English," I say for starters. "And after that, I can't read medicine, science, math, engineering, sentences that make their point with a formula here and there. And I can read but I don't read stories that were written centuries ago. If I were smarter, I would, but they bore me."

"Sleep is boring," Jeremy answers, after a spell. "Sleep bores me."

"Do you think so?" I ask him. "Really? Does it?" I am inside the scene and above it, watching the conversation as it happens, recording it, one shred of language at a time.

"Sleep bores me," Jeremy repeats, air between each

word. He turns his head and stares appreciatively through the window. He loses his grip on the spoon, and it falls: a metal kerplunk amid the abandoned cereal on the floor.

"Have you tried dreaming?" I ask him. "It's not as boring. It helps."

"I sleep with my eyes open," Jeremy reveals. "That way I know when it's morning."

IT TURNS OUT, after so many confounding years, that the words that eluded Jeremy in conversation became far more tangible, in his mind, when scrawled on boxes, paper, signs. At first I assumed it was Jeremy's indefatigable memory at work. When I would find him in his closet curled around a book, reciting the simple sentences in their order, I would conclude that he was repeating what he'd heard me say, raising his voice with the exclamation marks, pausing at the commas in imitation. *Vestiges of echolalia*, I thought, and though I did nothing to discourage his passion for books, I also did not allow myself to believe that Jeremy, then three and four years old, was really reading words. I took the same position regarding his intelligent assessment of signs: of course he knew what the metal octagons and rectangles instructed: STOP, YIELD, PEDESTRIAN CROSSING, NO PARKING. He loved cars, and he'd memorized the rules.

But Jeremy loved words, too; slowly, I started to see that. He had a genuine appreciation for their architecture, if not particularly for their application in everyday, run-of-the-mill exchanges. Sometime early in his fourth year, Jeremy began collecting intricate words and manipulating the internal sounds to see what would happen to the whole. Can*ta*loupe would become Can*won't*loupe. Water*me*lon was Water*smel*lon. Pinocchio's Jimi*ny* Cricket was renamed

Jimi*see* Cricket. It was an amusing game, blessedly weight-less and lighthearted, and all of us played—in the car, during meals, at the grocery store, on the deck. Word games became our family entertainment, a substitute for talk, and over time the games naturally evolved. One summer we focused on banishing pesky syllables by eliminating wedges from complex phrases, saying, for example: Remove the fifth syllable from the title *The Marvelous Journey Through the Night*, and what do you get? Answer: *The Marvelous Knee Through the Night*. Later that year, we pre-occupied ourselves with silly word combinations—cucumber pie, turkey lollipops, Thanksgiving goblins—some couplings striking Jeremy as so phenomenally preposterous that he would fall off his chair overcome, gasping for breath through his laughter.

Don't get me wrong: Jeremy's obsessions still crowded in against the games. Word twisters, language puzzles, books both relieved and provoked them. "You can have half of each," I would tell Jeremy sternly, when it was reading time. Half textbooks. Half stories. And then I would wait, listening as Jeremy's books tumbled off his shelves, as Jeremy cried in frustration, as another rash of badly behaved volumes fell to the floor before he would appear, several long minutes later, with a pile of books in his arms.

He would stack them on his bed where I was waiting. One tower of hardbound books with names like *More Great American Dream Machines*, *Classic Cars*, *The History of Chivalry and Armor*, and *Hunters in the Sky*. One far more modest display of paperbacks: *The Pig's Wedding*, *Friends*, *The Big Ball of String*. It was always the textbooks that captured Jeremy's imagination, extended captions to cutaway diagrams that would begin, "Just as Pontiac had their [*sic*] GTO and Oldsmobile their [*sic*] 442, Chevrolet had its little muscle car. The success of the GTO caught Chevrolet off guard." or, "The greater number of the nations who invaded the western empire termed the weapon *spada* or *spatha*, a name which, with various modifications, was retained in all the Romanesque languages." Jeremy barely had patience for the little watercolored tales, the innocent mischief of modern fables, but he would endure my dramatic readings of the paperbacks because he knew that a prized textbook was waiting in its tower. I took advantage of the situation by dwelling on character traits and plot lines— musing out loud about the adventures of pigs or the possibilities of a string or the unfortunate ensemble on a poor dog's head. My objective was to get Jeremy to care about the stories. To ask questions about the pig and the rooster, the mouse and the boy, the ridiculous conventions of puppies. To make extensions from their lives to his own. Empathy is a skill, we'd been told, that Jeremy would not naturally come by. No one had ever told us if it could indeed be taught, but if it could, I believed stories would prove to be the best instruction.

I DON'T KNOW when Jeremy crossed the line and started reading. I don't know how long he sat there and let me pretend that I knew something he didn't, let me go on as if I alone held the key to every book. I do know that Jeremy did everything he could to hide his new talent. He read in his closet, as I said. He shook his head furiously when I asked, "Have you been reading?" He looked away when I yawned and said, "I'm so sleepy. Can you read to me?" "You read," he would answer. "You read." And I didn't want to lose him, so I did.

I didn't get certain confirmation of Jeremy's reading talent until he was halfway through kindergarten at the country Quaker school. I was more than suspicious by then; Jeremy, in my company, had frequently blurted out a line or two—unscrambled a sign, puzzled over instructions on the computer screen, whispered along during my rendition of *Narnia*—but he'd always stopped short when he realized I was listening. He didn't want me to know. Someday, I plan to ask him why.

At school, however, Jeremy seemed more reconciled with his talent, and increasingly, during his first year there, I'd get reports from the principal, the administrator, the teacher, another mother, not just of Jeremy's facility with books but of his obvious allegiance to them as well. They comforted him, it was clear. They were the place he would go to when the classroom grew too noisy or when visitors overwhelmed him or when his hands wouldn't do the project set before him. When the second graders invaded the kindergarten room with a holiday parade, Jeremy grabbed a book and found the principal and settled into her tiny office to read. When a game didn't work out well or when Jeremy grew embarrassed, he turned to books to catch his breath and regain his ground. And in the afternoon, during the open-play hour, Jeremy began using books as paper bridges—reading to a younger boy in the private zone of the classroom loft, explaining a story to Saunders, teaching another boy, one his own age, the miracle of letters in return for a crayoned drawing of an automobile or a bus. The faster Jeremy could read words on paper, the faster words began to come to him in speech, and it wasn't long before Jeremy stood beside me in a pew at church and read, still hoping to avoid my notice, the printed Doxology, the

Apostles' Creed, the Affirmation of Faith. I dragged one finger under the words as if it were a selfish gesture, myself keeping myself in rhythm with the liturgy. But I wasn't speaking because Jeremy was, his voice small and distinctive in the pious Sunday crowd.

⌐

I WOULD LIKE to remember learning to read. I would like to again complete the puzzle for the very first time—to add a letter to a letter to a letter and to realize, suddenly, that I have stumbled upon a word, lurched into a new zone of language, opened the door. I would like to be thrown back once more by the thrill and the thrust of that surprise, to be blinded, like I must have been blinded, by type-bound words. But I can't remember the feeling. I can't return to that place in my mind, no matter how deeply I meditate, no matter how long I stand beneath the hot, pummeling water of the morning shower and spiral backward and backward in time. Did I make the discovery alone in my bed? Did my mother teach me? My brother? And what was happening outside—was there rain? was there sun?—when I found the key to my books?

I don't know the answers, nor do I know how it was for my son when he discovered the alluring mathematics of the alphabet. I have yet to understand how his mind works, how he accumulates data, how the invisible wires connect the bulbs in his brain, how the pulses of his intelligence are transferred, how he stores what he sees, how he recalls it, how he imagines, how he dreams. I don't know when Jeremy learned to read or how. I don't know if his body went hot, or if his heart started to pound, or if he had to close his eyes beneath the gold, gold light. I am saying, I suppose, that after all these years Jeremy is still a mystery to me, and yet, at last, something concrete has begun to build between us. These confounding words, these fragile conversations, these nascent questions, these inquiries at a kitchen table in a slant of sun. There are words between us now. Language. It's the secret I share with my son.

from here to there

*I*sn't it strange," Jeremy asks me, "how you get from here to there?" We're baking cookies on a lovely spring afternoon, have already tasted more of the dough than is proper. By the time my husband gets home, we'll be in no mood for dinner, but I emphatically don't care. Jeremy and I are talking, and everything else is secondary.

"What do you mean?" I hurry to follow the line of his thinking. "Which here and which there are you considering?" I turn toward him and I'm in time to catch his eye. I look into him for a moment before he looks away.

"I mean first I was in New Life. Then I was with Miss Tara. Now I'm a real kindergartner. How does it happen? How do you get from here to there?" Jeremy darts his eyes away and starts pacing, his feet clopping down on the vinyl floor, his fingers forming his own brand of sign language. It appears as if he were pulling letters from the air, physically pushing his thoughts all around as he finds one word after the other.

"Boy," I answer him, "that's a tough one, Jeremy. Time must feel like magic to you, but what is happening is that we're growing bit by bit. Day by day. We make decisions. We get bigger. We make new friends. Do different things."

"Yup," Jeremy says, nodding, possibly to stop me from talking. "Because I remember things. I remember Miss Janie and Miss Janie's house. I went there thirty times, maybe thirty-one. I went there more Wednesdays than Thursdays." He stops, looks at me quickly, keeps pacing. I have my back to the oven. The first tray of cookies is no doubt burning.

"You had fun there," I smile, stopping to think: thirty-one visits sounds about right. "Miss Janie really loves you."

"Yup. I had fun. Wasn't Timmy funny? Who do you think was funnier? Timmy or me?" For Jeremy this is a serious question, and I consider all the alternatives before answering.

"Well, Jeremy, I think you were both pretty cool. I can't really say who was funnier."

"I think Timmy," Jeremy declares. He's clopping so exuberantly across the kitchen floor that his socks have extended way past his toes. I think about leaning over to straighten him up, but that would interfere with his thought, so I do nothing. "Timmy liked costumes. I didn't. That makes Timmy funnier."

"You liked race-car helmets," I suggest.

"That's not a costume," Jeremy corrects me. "That's a hat."

"Oh."

"So I don't know for sure if Timmy was funnier, but now I live in another place and we don't see Timmy and I'm in kindergarten. It's funny, getting from here to there."

"Is that okay with you?" I ask. "All those changes?"

"Yup."

"Do you like this house?" I ask.

"Yup." Jeremy's still walking back and forth, and I know he's not agreeing to like the house out of politeness. Across the board, he calls things as he sees them. Matter-of-factly, he continues: "This house is in a different neighborhood. It doesn't have all the same nice colors. Do you remember the other house?"

"Yes," I tell him. "I do. I remember it well."

"It used to be gray," Jeremy says. "Then it got painted by George. That was when I was interested in trains and knights. Both things. Isn't that funny?"

"What?" For an instant, I'm confused by the sequence of thoughts.

"Having two interests. At the same time. Trains and knights."

"You're allowed," I tell him. "It's okay to like two things at once." The cookies are definitely burning now, but this is too exceptional to disrupt.

"But it's not as much fun," Jeremy says. "Definitely not. It's better when you only like one thing at once."

JEREMY IS GONE after that. It's been a huge and, I'm sure, taxing conversation, and now he's taken his pacing out to the hallway. Not interfering is the reward I give him for sharing so many deep thoughts with me. Pretty soon I hear him say, "Mommy, I'm going outside."

"That's fine," I say. "But what do you need?" I'm washing the dishes at the sink, make the mistake of not going out to address him directly, as I've begun to learn that I should. Unless I directly oversee the completion of some basic tasks, Jeremy will get lost in his shuffle.

"What do you mean?" he calls, a little agitated.

"What do you need to go outside?" I call back.

"What?" he asks.

"You need your shoes," I tell him. "You can't go outside without shoes."

"Oh! My shoes!" he says. "Shoes. Shoes. Shoes."

I wait for several moments before I say another word, peek out of the kitchen to the hallway, where he is. Jeremy's still pacing up and down. It's become a skipping, free-form pace, almost dancelike in its contortions. At the end of each line, Jeremy does a hopping about-face turn and smiles to himself, as if he'd just seen paradise. "Shoes on yet?" I ask.

"My what?" Jeremy says, after a few minutes.

"Your shoes. Do you have them on?"

"Oh! My shoes!"

Jeremy keeps pacing, and finally I shut the faucet off, go out to the hallway, and put my hands on his shoulders. "Have you decided not to go outside?" I ask him.

"What?" He shrugs off my light touch.

"Don't you need your shoes?"

"Oh yeah! My shoes! I keep forgetting." I stand and supervise—like I always end up doing—until Jeremy's got his Velcro-fastened sneakers on, and now he's finally outside, where I can watch him from the window. He doesn't play with the ball or the toy jeep or the wooden plane; he heads directly for a new round of pacing. Pacing is one of Jeremy's passions, and I'm only just now learning how to deal with it. I know that if I don't let him pace at all, he grows edgy and frantic, unable to focus, darker in spirit, not as flexible as he can be, hardly approachable. If I let it go on too long, he becomes equally irretrievable, starts pacing faster and faster; the word that always comes to mind is *manic*. I try my best to keep him on middle ground, somewhere between where he's inclined to go and where I would like to see him. No one's ever offered any guidelines on the pacing issue. I keep making things up as I go, trying not to worry what the neighbors might think about the grassless patch in our front yard. At Jeremy's school, I've shared my pacing philosophy with his teachers, who agree to give him some room during recess and free play, but to urge him into the mainstream all other times. There are periods when Jeremy's more resistant to guidance, more difficult to extrude from his own mind, more determined to pace and pace and pace. But Jeremy's teachers and I are getting used to these cycles, try to ease one another out of despair when we see him sliding too far away. *He's just going through a hard time*, we tell one another. Or, *He's working something complicated out in his head. Whenever he solves whatever it is, he will most certainly be back.*

Recently, though, Jeremy's been in a communicative phase, offering more of himself than ever before. He's coming up with the most marvelous metaphors, letting me in on little secrets he's been keeping. I feel perpetually on the edge of myself, all senses keen toward him, ready—at the smallest sign—to stop whatever I'm doing and encourage his indulgence. Lately he's grown aware that there are jokes in the world, and he's been trying out his own mix on me—deliberately misconstruing some facts that he knows and presenting the mismatch in a single joking sentence. "Guess what, Mommy?" "What?" "They flew the F-14s in World War II."

Along with Jeremy's budding sense of humor has come a sophisticated understanding of relative weights and balances. There is what is fair and what is not: "I try harder, but he does it better." Or, "Daddy's the best artist in the world, but they don't put his work in a museum." There is what matters in the long run, a calculation Jeremy has made entirely on his own. "Mommy, do you know what's true? Being a nice person is the most important thing. Some kids are good at things but they're not good at being nice. Being nice is hardest. Being nice is the most important thing."

Maybe because we're spending more time in church, Jeremy's also been musing about higher powers. He has, for example, decided that God drives a jeep across the sky, a huge off-road vehicle equipped to handle cumulus clouds. I don't care how often he's already mentioned this, it strikes me as fabulous each time. His concept of God seems far beyond his years; I am surprised, continually, by what he says. He'll come to me, for example, when I'm not feeling well and say, "Don't worry, Mommy. We all get old, but that's okay because when we die we get to walk around in heaven. And everybody who's already dead will be there so you won't even have to be lonely." I'll tell him it's just a migraine and that I'm not going anywhere, and then he'll kiss me gratefully on the nose and say, "Do you think God can see us right now?" I'll tell Jeremy that I'm not sure of much in life, but I definitely see God through his eyes. God is watching.

⟜

WHEN THE COOKIES are out of the oven, I call Jeremy back to the house, try teasing him in with the one uncharred specimen of melting chocolate chips. "No thanks," he says politely. "I don't want a cookie."

"I really do want you back in the house," I say. "I think you've been pacing long enough." I stand at the door and watch him. He looks up, but only briefly, at me.

"Five more minutes," he bargains. Does a hop, skip, turns, runs a jagged line.

"Okay. Five minutes. And then we'll play a game," I tell him. A neighbor drives by. I wave. This scene is familiar to them.

"I don't want to play a game," Jeremy says, getting agitated.

"A puzzle, then," I suggest. "We'll do a puzzle."

"You said five minutes." Jeremy's firm about that. "I need five more minutes."

"Okay," I say. "But I'm serious."

⟶

IT TAKES TEN minutes to get Jeremy back in the house. He's a little discombobulated, but he soon pulls through. "I don't want to do a puzzle," he tells me. "They're boring." He wrinkles his nose.

I frankly have no desire to do a puzzle, either, right now, but I have to find something enticing. "How about Tell a Story?" I suggest. "Chutes and Ladders? Sand art?"

"Boring," Jeremy tells me.

"How about a story hour? You can choose the books. We can even do textbooks, if you want to."

"We already did that," Jeremy complains. "That would be boring."

"How about sitting and talking?" I ask, knowing full well that whatever I suggest will be dubbed boring. "We have to do something, because I don't want any more pacing. You've had enough for the day."

"Okay," he says grudgingly. I put my hand under his chin and ask him to please look at me. Reluctantly he does. We sit at the table in perfect silence for a too-long minute. I try to start a few conversations, but they seem inconsequential. Soon I stop. After another spell of sitting and staring, Jeremy gets tears in his eyes.

"Hey," I say. "What's wrong? I didn't mean to upset you."

"Nothing," Jeremy says. "Nothing's wrong."

"But something is," I say, pursuing it. "You're starting to cry." I stroke his head but it doesn't help. I wage a brief war with myself about pacing. Why didn't I wait until he was ready to come inside? Why didn't I simply and gratefully acknowledge that he'd already given me a big piece of himself, and now needed more time than usual to restore his sense of balance?

"It's just that my eyes feel funny," Jeremy says. "But my body's not sad." The tears catch on his lashes before sliding down his cheek and turning the corner at his chin. He brushes them away with his hands.

"I just didn't want you to keep pacing, Jeremy," I apologize. "I don't think it's good for you. You get stuck if you pace too long. But we'll think of something. I promise. It doesn't have to be awful." I lift Jeremy out of his seat and pull him as close to me as I can, embrace him, settle my chin onto his shoulder. We stay like this for a long time, while in my mind I click down a list of alternatives.

"Mommy," Jeremy says, breaking into my thinking, "how are we supposed to see God?" He sobs after he asks the question, and I wonder if this is what he has been outside contemplating. Is this what has been going on in his mind?

"What do you mean, Jeremy?" I ask him, pulling back so that I can see his face. "What do you mean by *suppose?*"

"How are we supposed to see Him?" Jeremy repeats, using his fingers again, to help him through this. He tries not to cry, makes an o with his lips, tilts his head back to prevent stray tears from falling.

"God's all around us," I tell him. "God made things special. God's in the beauty of things."

"But," Jeremy sobs, "they put the dead bodies in the ground and the spirits don't have eyeballs, so how are you supposed to see God when you're already dead?" He's getting sadder and sadder in my arms. He presses up against me, and I fold him in.

"Oh my little boy," I say. "You worry about such grown-up things." I fight back my own tears now. It hurts tremendously to not have the answers.

"I just want to know," he tells me. "I just want to know. Because I really, really do want to see God. It would be interesting to know what He looks like."

I don't know what to say. We sit there doing nothing, not talking, in the fading scent of the baked chocolate chip cookies. After a while Jeremy senses that I'm not merely being silent; I'm dumbfounded. Like the little miracle that he is, like the empathetic child he has indisputably become, he knows as well that he's saddened me. Untangling himself from my arms, he finds my lips and kisses me gently. "It's okay, Mommy," he tells me, still fighting back his own wayward crying. "Even if you don't know yet, I love you."

harm's way

I have an imperfect memory. My mind is out of balance, naturally predisposed, I think, to haunt itself with terrors. So that what I remember of childhood are the things that scared me, while my brother and sister remember the fun. I remember the things I wish I hadn't done, the things I saw too soon, the evil interactions, though there were, comparatively, far more sweet ones. Fears, anxieties don't die with me, they hardly get diminished, and it has therefore been my lot to fight them into a place that only I can see so that others do not sense my panic, don't have to live it the way I do, day after day, an entire lifetime.

As a mother, the fears inside me multiply and heighten for all the obvious reasons, and then some. Fears for my son's health and heart, fears for his future, fears about doctors and treatments and the stunning lack of cures, fears, the recurrent question: *Am I big enough, strong enough, smart enough for this?* But mostly fear of the world my son is stepping into: this planet of people and madness and houses that hardly contain us, rules that barely guide us, primordial instincts, vulgarity, dishonesty—perhaps the highest crime of which I, my only child's mother, helper, friend, have at times been guilty. *Protect my son*, I pray at night, but then God must also protect my son from me.

And from the school yard. From places over which, increasingly, I have no jurisdiction. *Treat him just like any other student,* I tell his teachers, defiantly, and then I scurry them into a corner and advise them to take particular care in regard to this sort of situation, that brand of peril. *He'll walk beneath the swings; don't let him,* I caution. *He'll wander out of the gates with a thought fixed in his mind. Watch him on the streets. Please.* I want the teachers to stop, make sure he's safe. I want them to act like nothing's different. I want them to sanctify this part of his life and make sure it turns out perfect. I want—face the fact—the impossible. *Be his friend,* I tell them. *Really,* touching their shoulder reassuringly. But what does that actually mean?

Throughout the school day, when Jeremy's gone, I worry myself crazy, superimposing my anxieties over story hour, circle time, arts and crafts, snacks, recess. I imagine him raising his hand and trying to speak and not having the words that are needed, simply halting—right there, presentence—while the other children titter behind their hands. I imagine him grappling with his crayons and scribbling his colors way out of bounds, working his lower lip and his brow, concentrating, doing his mighty, mighty best. I imagine him lying on the free-play carpet above a box of toy cars and letting nobody into his game, inciting a riot among five-year-olds who can't possibly understand his parking garages and highway traffic, his emergencies and fantasies, his impulse to be alone. Worst, I imagine him getting ready for recess, struggling with his zipper and his hood, standing last in line in his own small society, then running, tripping behind the others into the wind. He is not strong enough for the tricycles or the miniature monkey bars. He won't understand the reciprocality of hide-

and-seek, house and store, cowboys and Indians, policemen and thieves. He will not know what the old log balance beam is for, and he will sit in its middle, looking up at the sky, thinking his thoughts while the planet spins and his classmates run around him, call his name, prod him with their fingers, ask—no, now they are making small demands—that he give them their balance beam back.

WARNINGS HAVE NO influence, most of the time. Mud slides, earthquakes, meteors just happen, and if you're standing there, if one fault in the earth finally crumbles to its knees or one speck of a dead star ruptures out of its orbit and falls, falls, falls toward your feet, no amount of motherly precaution will see you through. You can be counseled, *Take an umbrella*, but the entire sky might open. You can be told, *Don't talk to strangers*, but it's up to you to sift through faces. You can be exhorted, *Don't drive past limits*, but perhaps the speed of your car is the sole thing that saved you from the buck galloping out of the forest. You can remember the rape on the movie screen, fear your own body, hang like a shadow against the dance-hall walls, but if a man decides what some men will, if a man rattles the door to your hotel room free, if a man waits on your bed while you carelessly sing in the hot white smoke of a midday shower, no lessons can save you. Only your fists can. Only the lamp behind the intruder's head and a scream that blisters out of the room, under the door, all up and down the hallway of the tall, unnaturally white hotel.

I drive my son to school and attempt to teach him lessons. "Talk to the other kids," I tell him. "Let them be your friends." Reconsidering, I add, "You don't have to be friends if someone happens to be mean. Really. What's the point?"

I philosophize—more obfuscation—about bikes. "Try one of those Big Wheels at recess today, Jeremy," I encourage. "It could be fun. Take a chance," I goad him. "How could it hurt? Can't hurt, I promise, except listen to me, listen: Don't you dare go near the street. Stay out of the road, will you, Jeremy? If you decide to ride a bike." Talking as I drive, fumbling over the lessons, knowing that this is the easiest part, that in a few years or so, the topic du jour will be peer pressure and deadly poisons—subjects on which I have even less expertise.

Things happen. They are bound to, and they do. No mother, no teacher, no playground supervisor can wage an assault against the inevitable. For a little boy diagnosed with obsessions and aloneness, life is an unusual peril, and for the parents, for me, taking responsibility means facing a boggle of bad choices. Do I teach my son to be afraid before he has summoned the courage to trust? Do I counsel caution before he is willing to take a risk? Do I enumerate dangers, do I hide them? Do I urge self-defense before he can possibly know what battles are worth his fists, his heart, his soul?

SEVERAL WEEKS AGO, I picked Jeremy up from his school. His eyes were hooded and he wasn't talking, but that isn't so unusual and I let it go. Between his school and our house lie twenty-five minutes of farmlands and nurseries, horses, estates, long-necked geese, and we drove with the radio on, me singing along, Jeremy perched rigid as a rail on the passenger's side. At traffic lights, I'd lean to my right to bring Jeremy closer, but like a stranger, he'd recoil at my touch— backing himself into the corner of our modest car. "Hey, you okay?" I asked him gently, and he shook his head furiously, affirmatively: *Don't ask again.* We weren't into our driveway before his seat belt was off. We had barely come to a stop when he was gone—slamming the car door behind him and escaping to the side of our yard, where he began to run laps, his head low, his eyes on his shoes, his light-weight jacket twisting madly behind him. "Do you want a snack?" I called to him helplessly, and he answered, "Leave me alone!" So I sat on our deck and I watched him storm and wondered what had gone wrong. I'd never seen quite this degree of wrath in Jeremy. Never seen anger this color, so much like hatred.

I couldn't stop the fury. It went on all afternoon, and whenever I left the deck and circled near Jeremy, tried to settle him down with the weight of my hands, with firm, instructive words, he reared: "Don't touch me!" Finally, at dusk, I fought him to the ground, carried him—raging—inside, locked the deck door, stood before it, hollered back at him: "Tell me! Tell me what is wrong!" But he couldn't answer. His heart was too cluttered, his language too imprecise to convey whatever desperate truth he'd come by.

It wasn't an easy night. Jeremy was black-eyed and angry before assenting, ferociously, to bed, and he punched his feet against the plaster wall throughout the night, before falling off to sleep. For days Jeremy wasn't himself—wouldn't let me near him, would not converse, would not reveal anything to me—and I, not understanding what it was that had gone wrong, fell back on bad habits and blamed his turn of heart on me. I looked inward and worried until one unfamiliar angel approached me at an end-of-school picnic several days after the disturbance had first appeared. "I just want to know," this woman told me, "whether your son is better now."

"Better than what?" I asked her, stepping back. She was

the mother of one of Jeremy's classmates, but I hardly knew her. What did she know? What could she?

"Better than the other day," she continued, confused, it was clear, by my question. "My son . . ." She paused, considered. "My son was devastated."

"By what?" I asked her, my eyes filling, my heart jumping up in my throat.

"On the playground," the mother told me, cautiously. She was honest, genuinely concerned. "You know: the fight. The other kids. The ones who pushed your son around."

"Who pushed my son around?" I could barely get the words out. "Why?"

"My son spoke of little else that afternoon," the woman answered, perplexed by my lack of information, too far into her story now to retract it, to make it go away. "My son was sorry it happened," she continued. "He had wanted to get Jeremy free."

"Of what?" I insisted, as if I hadn't heard her the first time. "Free of what?"

"It had something to do with a balance beam," the woman reconstructed. "It was part of some game that the others were playing, and Jeremy, as I understand it, wouldn't move from his seat on the beam."

"So?" I asked, closing my eyes, not wanting to imagine. "So what happened?"

"So they pushed him," she said. "Or so I take it. Four or five of them."

"Oh," I said, crumbling. "Oh."

"When he started to run, the kids pushed him harder, chased him, I guess. I think it got ugly. I think he was scared. My son, two other boys, they were the ones who alerted the adults. They were over the hill, just had their backs turned, for that instant. They were on it right away, of course. It was over almost as soon as it had started."

"Oh," I said. "Oh."

"He didn't mention it?" my son's friend's mother asked, after a silence. "I was sure he would have. Something like that?"

"No. Or yes. Yes, actually. I think he's been telling me all week long. I just didn't have a way to hear him."

"Oh," she said. "I'm sorry. I wasn't trying to upset you."

"No."

"I was just trying to say . . ."

"What?"

"That my son is sorry. It frightened him, too. He's been talking about it for days."

A little boy, I thought. *A five-year-old innocence eroded.* "Tell your son thank you, for me," I said. "Will you? Thank him for fighting on my son's behalf."

"I will," she said. "I have already."

"Good."

"I've thanked him."

"That's good."

"Are you okay?"

"Yes. Actually: No. I need to talk to Jeremy. I need to . . . Some things, I haven't explained."

"It's hard on all of us," the woman offered, edging back now, touching my shoulder before she walked away. "Boys' games. Growing up. It becomes so very hard."

➤

I TOOK JEREMY shopping that afternoon. I told him he could have anything he wanted; I had a plastic card. But it was clear he'd rather play at home, and so we drove in that direction with the music low—sad songs on a folk-song station. I kept assembling words in my head, but they were insubstantial, and finally, all I could put forth, an offering, was, "I heard about what happened on the playground, Jeremy. It had to be real scary, and I'm sorry."

"Mommy?" Jeremy answered, after a long spell of staring out the window, fidgeting with his seat belt, struggling, mid-sentence, with language.

"Yes?"

"Mommy, I was scared."

"I know, little guy." I reached out my hand to his hand. "I get scared, too, just thinking about it." And I do, I do—putting myself in that wrathful circle, feeling the thumping of unrestrained fists, fighting the yank of a small human knot, and unable, for just an instant, to see blue sky. I can't breathe when I imagine this. I can't survive the possibility—no, the fact—that it has happened, and that it will happen again, to my son.

"Mommy?"

"Yes?"

"Other kids, they tried to help me. They got the grown-ups. They made it stop."

"They're good friends," I said. "They're very special."

"They stopped it," Jeremy answered. "And I was scared." He shifted leftward in the passenger seat, closer to me than he had been for days, trusting me at last with his sorrow, with this huge, indelible thing he had learned about sitting on a split-log beam in pleasant recess weather. I turned the radio off and imagined his rescue—imagined three little boys bearing witness, feeling helpless, maybe pounding the backs of the aggressors with their own fists, before running to find the some help. Scant screen of forest on either side, my son now tucked safely under my arm, I listened to the sound of our breathing—small, uneven exchanges of air—while the tires rumbled distantly beneath us. *What can I offer?* I wondered. *What can I say that will be a comfort and a truth, that will protect him, that will guide him, that will strengthen his position in this world?* "Friends matter," I told him, finally, the only lesson I could draw.

blindsided

*E*arlier tonight it was my idea to grab some dinner at a nearby fast-food dive. It was just the two of us, my husband being tied up with work downtown, and we didn't have much to celebrate, save for the passing of a storm. "It's like a date, and you won't have to eat my cooking," I'd said to win Jeremy over, and he'd shrugged agreement and we were off. By 6:30, we'd parked the car. By 6:45, we'd moved through the line, paid the nose-earringed teen, and found our place among the crowd of somber diners. We chose a corner table near the entranceway and sat facing the street, looking out upon the avenue, the chintzy shops, Best Auto Tag. We were watching the patrons come and go—the sweaters thrown over thin tee-shirts, the untied Keds, the end-of-day hair, the sagging briefcases. We were sitting catercornered to each other, sharing mashed potatoes, chicken, buttered corn, speaking of monkey bars and how it feels to hang from steel, and I felt safe and whole with Jeremy, and he felt safe with me. That's how it was. I wasn't thinking. I'd left my stalwart vigilance at home.

It was the sunset hour, and though we didn't have much of a skyscape view, we were aware of the pinkening chrome of cars, of the fireballs of reflective light, surfaces receding.

Partway through dinner we started playing a familiar game—counting the luxury cars on the avenue and making claims about their owners: what other cars they had at home, how it felt to drive in style. A dark green Lexus was headed west, in our direction, and Jeremy cast out his thought-through theories while I devised my own, and then, a surprise, the Lexus slowed into a right-hand turn and parked in the angled spot beside our car. People who drive luxury cars don't usually dine where we were dining, and Jeremy and I had a laugh about that. When a Jaguar traveling east caught Jeremy's eye, he moved on to other speculations. I stayed with the Lexus a second longer, and that's when I saw what I saw. A woman unlike any I had ever imagined, her face not a face but two flesh domes joined at right angles. On one of those domes she had a squint of an eye; on the other she had nothing at all.

I lowered my head and covered my eyes, and said a prayer for what would happen next. As calmly as I could, I leaned in Jeremy's direction and told him firmly, "I need you to understand that something scary is about to happen. Listen to me carefully and you won't need to get upset." I closed my eyes again, took a deep breath, and tried to formulate the right explanation.

I could hear Jeremy's fork drop on his plate, and I could feel the pull of his hand on my hand, sensed the heat of him, the demand for an explanation, *now*. I looked up and his eyes were all over me, his face already red, his heart thumping visibly in his fragile, shallow chest. "Mommy?" he asked me. "Mommy?" *Go on*. The voice in me. *Tell him*. The utter lack of intelligent words. "Listen, Jeremy, these are the facts: In a few minutes, a man and a lady are going to walk up those steps and come through that door, go to the line, and order dinner. They're going to sit here in this

room with us, because probably they're hungry. The
woman isn't feeling well and it might upset you to see her.
It will make her sad if she sees you afraid, it will make her
feel terribly lonely. We can't do that. We can't let it happen.
So what we're going to do instead is you keep talking, you
keep eating, you look right at me. Don't stare out the window until I say you can. Then, when I tell you, look out the
window again and point to the first luxury vehicle you see.
Tell me its story. Make it up. You've been doing great so
far."

Jeremy flushed another shade of red. He made that
trembling white circle with his lips that he makes when
he's determined not to cry. Blindly he reached for his fork
and blindly he stabbed at his plate, swallowing air most of
the time because the corn was clopping to the floor like yellow rain. All the while he continued looking at me and I
kept looking at him, though out of the corner of one eye, I
saw the couple approaching, climbing—in a tremulous
way—the concrete steps that led to the entrance door.

I tried to think. I tried to flash back to all the times something like this had happened before, wished for the mil-
lionth time that Jeremy had not seen what he had in fact
seen when he was five years old, when a teacher's aid
unwrapped a bandage to show off a fresh surgical scar. The
unveiling sent Jeremy into cutting terror from which he has
not yet recovered. He didn't go to preschool for several days
after that, clung to me, hid his eyes in my shoulder, and he's
been walking through crowds wary and nervous ever since,
testing everything first with his peripheral vision.

These days Jeremy has more than the regular shyness for
the misproportioned entity, the asymmetry induced by a
scar, a wound. To him it's incomprehensible and therefore
alarming that a man could lose the flesh below the hip, or

that a woman could slump in a wheelchair, concave with thinness and age. Eyes made twice their human size by the fractured glare of bifocals disturb him. Band-Aids do. The hard white sleeve of a cast throws the balance off, and him. In these years as Jeremy's mother, I have learned how to be wary—how to go out into crowds a perpetual two steps ahead so as to reconnoiter, assess the risks, and steer a sheltered path. I have turned my child left or right, hooded his eyes with my hand, drummed up distractions, shuffled and careened, all in an effort to circumvent the off encounter, to avoid frightening him, to refrain from disturbing or embarrassing the person he would be unstrung by. It is not a perfect methodology—there have been enormous failures—and now that Jeremy is navigating more of this world on his own, I understand that my protective shield is shadow-thin, and fading.

Jeremy and I were sitting in the corner, but we were also sitting near the door and sitting directly along the path that the couple would have to take in order to place their order and pay. Only seconds would elapse, in other words, between the time the couple would mount the steps and the time they would brush by us, but it felt now as if the clock had jammed. I was holding Jeremy's hand, half watching the progress on the steps, monitoring the door, whispering, "Now, Jeremy. Now. You look outside and find a winner. Find me a Z3 or a Rover. Point it out. I want a beauty." Squalling all the while at me, giving myself directives: *You look at her, Beth. You smile at her. Let her know she's welcome here.*

The chimes clattered on the door when the husband pushed it open. The hinges squealed as the door fell back into place. Jeremy hadn't found his luxury car, but he was focusing fiercely on the window, and now it was up to me to

finish the job, to show a face of calm and everyday welcome
to the courageous domed woman and the accompanying
man. Straightening my spine, blowing out some air, I
turned at just enough of an angle to acknowledge how the
husband had draped an arm across his wife's shoulders, like
a wing, how he had fixed his other arm into a ledge, a
branch for her to hold on to. I noticed her hands taking on
that ledge, an arch like music in her delicate fingers. I
noticed the proportions of her, the tight breasts, the slender
waist, the very tiny ankles above a pair of tennis shoes. I
tried to look above her neck, to lift my eyes to her one eye,
to smile pleasantly enough, but now the man and the
woman were coming closer, nearing our table, taking their
turn, and there was only a split second left, and what I
needed then was time. More time, more spine to halt the
mutiny of my own best intentions, to perform a simple,
human act. I needed, wanted, prayed for time in the wrath
of this eternity, but then the gates of chance were closing,
my eyes weren't budging, the couple turned, went by.
"BMW!" Jeremy reported, at a nervous volume, and I
wrenched abruptly, stared at the streetscape, felt the heat of
shame in my face. If we are one another's mirrors, then I'd
just reflected horror, and how can that be overlooked in an
already dangerous world?

Like Jeremy, I started stabbing at my plate, an impotent
facsimile of normal. I spoke too loudly about the cars outside, conversed with awful animation. Soon I understood
that the air behind us was collapsing slowly, and now there
was a hush, and now a silence, so that only the overhead
music continued playing unaffected. Chairs started screech-
ing against the tiled floor. A child in another corner cried.
A family stood up from their unfinished dinner and headed
for the door. Still, the man and his wife continued toward

the counter, pressed on, and now another couple made a hasty exit, and now an old man wheezed his way outside. On the concrete steps, five teenage boys had congregated, were slouching upward in too-grand pants and attitudes, a hip night out on the town, until the first among them caught a view through the window and froze. A gesture with his chin, and then the friends behind him froze, did not step forward, began to slink away. They retreated to the edge of the parking lot and lit up smokes. The door chimes clattered one more time, and now it was the boy who'd served Jeremy and me our chicken—already a cigarette plopped in his mouth, a cap quickly pulled down on his head.

Jeremy was controlled but breathing hard, his body shaking. I took both of his hands in mine, then pulled him closer, and then, with him secure against my chest, I turned my head and bore witness to the back side of the couple, the part of them that I could now, from my safe distance, see. I noticed her hair this time, how pretty it was, a glittering color. I noticed how she was leaning into him, how he was pulling her closer. Above her left shoulder, the massive, eyeless dome of flesh extended sideways and sideways, and its skin looked touchable and soft, looked like the hairless head of an infant. I noticed, again, the man's deliberate, gentle wing. I saw the tenderness between them, the secret histories of their bodies. *In sickness and in health:* those words I saw. *In sickness.* They were standing there at the chicken counter, earning a meal together, a night in the world after the passing of a storm. They were wanting no more than to sit down unnoticed, and finally, finally, the manager came and took their order.

There is no hero at the end of this story. There is no moment when the hostile fear of that restaurant is ruptured with a gesture, a hello. There is no second chance, no mercy, no taking away what we have—all of us—done: a conspiracy of silence, victimization. There is no lesson that I have taught my son that I want him to remember, no part of me that does not at this instant feel unholy, unclean, indecent. It is frankly unforgivable that I, who know the brutality of differentness and the loneliness of separateness, could not, did not extend beyond myself. We are thrown together on a temporary planet, and the only thing we have to protect ourselves from the fury of our fate is kindness incarnate, small acts of grace. This is what I tell my son later, after the fact, when it's too late. When we are already driving home in the fallen evening, and the man and his wife are seated alone, in the fast-food restaurant.

what falls away

Kindergarten is over now, and no one is wondering about the fall. No one has asked us for fresh test scores; I'm not in the promise-making business. Jeremy will return to the school in the country, where he knows the terrain, has visited first grade, has a head start on a few true friendships. A boy named James. A boy named Will. Girls with big bows in their hair. It's early June, and Jeremy speaks of his friends, declares he is already missing his classmates. He takes the calendar off the refrigerator door and begins to suggest some play dates, and then he's formulating lists of the things he and his guests might do—Monopoly, Scratch-Art, go out to lunch, don't touch the cars. He writes everything down on a fat sheaf of paper in handwriting that slopes gently down a hill, then runs a tight circle around me while I make calls. When a play date is established, he pumps his fist in the air. "Yes," he says. "Yes. Oh, I can't wait. Let's buy James some bagels." In a few weeks Jeremy will be at camp six hours a day—a near-perfect situation that will rotate him through science, geography, selected sports, art, swimming, creative expression. He'll be taken care of by counselors who are enormously positive and nurturing, men and women who made him feel right at home during his orientation tour—they'd taken his hand, walked him through things, answered his important questions as if they'd been old friends for life. He'll be looked after by a staff of educators that exalts diversity, provides assistance when a child needs assistance, refuses to leave a child on the outer rim. It's the kind of place I wish I'd known of years ago. The kind of place I hope there's more of soon.

But at the moment time has no boundaries or restrictions, and Jeremy's making the most of his freedom. We're everywhere. We go to the city, to the parks, to the mall, to my mother's; every afternoon, no matter what, we walk for an hour in the dappling light of the sun. We call it a nature walk, but it's just the neighborhood we're touring, just worms we find, a colony of ants, a bird watching hungrily from a tree. Invigorated by a nascent self-confidence, Jeremy nevertheless lets me hold his hand. Offers it to me, and I take it gladly, lean toward him, give him a kiss. He's absolutely growing up. Next year, the year after, our walks will not be quite like this. Jeremy will be running ahead. I'll be standing behind. Raising a prayer of gratitude to heaven.

IT SEEMS TO me that the stronger Jeremy grows, the more confounding becomes the incipient question: *Just what has happened here?* Five years ago we saw our child disappearing—a rapid descent into silence. We met with doctors. We were given terminology. The terminology was a dark room, a dead end, an imbroglio not an enlightenment. *Pervasive developmental disorder not otherwise specified* is a label extended to tens of thousands of children. It is a term one hears with increasing frequency; part of the shared lexicon of therapists, recent special-education graduates, bewildered parents. It's an active search on the Internet. But it remains, in my mind, nothing more than a cipher, a way of saying, *We are not quite sure what's wrong.*

In the absence of medical understanding, a proven therapy, a crystal ball, my husband and I looked to love as the only possible solution. Began at the beginning with a fierceness of heart and a rock-hard unwillingness to regard our son as anything less than what we knew he inherently was. Training our vision on the things we believed most mattered, we built and sustained an idiosyncratic household in which obeying a bedtime, finishing the food on one's plate, cleaning one's room after play, learning to brush one's teeth or to dress oneself or to tie one's shoes or to exercise one's please-and-thank-you-wait-until-I'm-finished manners all failed to get much notice. Juxtaposed against the imperative that Jeremy regain his language and feel safe in the world, the customary family rituals seemed piddling and irrelevant. Communication had to come first. We weren't going anywhere until Jeremy could express the complex thoughts that filled his head, and we leaned on love, we leaned on the innate courage of our child to see us through.

This meant that at first our house whirled and rumbled with windy monologues—me thinking my every thought out loud so that Jeremy would not lose touch with the sound of words, their melodies. Me telling stories. Me reading stories. Me playing music. Me commenting on the weather or the tragic state of political affairs. Me explaining in excruciating detail what we were going to buy at the gift store and why. It meant that at the end of every day my husband would take Jeremy in his arms and whisper to him stories of his own—secret tales about growing up in the mountains of El Salvador, a joke about an aunt who'd kept a pet monkey on a chain.

But it also meant that when Jeremy's words slowly started to resurface, we stepped back, listened intently, and extended *his* words in every possible direction. We rhymed them. We wrote them down. We made up songs that evoked the spoken sentiment. We picked up the phone and got Grandmom on the line, because we knew she'd be as delighted as we were. Tried out half sentences on the friendly grocery-store clerk. Typed letters to an uncle and an aunt. Ran across the drive to our neighbor, who listened to Jeremy with the kind of reverence she'd give to a Mozart or a Bach. Like new settlers in a land of trees, we cleared a space for Jeremy's language, insisted that he be listened to, would not allow a soul to interrupt him while he haltingly searched for his words. No matter what Jeremy was saying, no matter how many times he might have already said it, no matter how long it was taking him to get from the first word to the second, we gave him room, didn't shut him down, let the dinner burn if the dinner had to burn, didn't pay attention to the phone, didn't answer the doorbell, stayed up past a reasonable bedtime, if that's what it took to ensure opportunity for self-expression. When Jeremy started talking, we made certain that he had the audience he deserved.

We were, I admit, raising Jeremy to put his faith in what for a very long while was a predominantly adult world. Adults were the ones who would stop and listen, who wouldn't run right by him, who would give him a chance to speak his mind, who would admire what he loved without disturbing it. We transported him to other places, therefore, included him in all our conversations, sat him down with friends of ours and helped him through small conversations. It was, we knew, an artificial construct, but it was meeting the world halfway, controlling the speed at which we let real life in. More than once we had seen our son shut down in the face of what he interpreted as overwhelming social pressure. Too painfully, we had witnessed what could happen in a household of brute insensitivity, individuals like the mother of that "genius" girl who, Jeremy most likely sensed at the time, was not kind and could not possibly befriend him. We would not go that way again. We developed a philosophy of gradual reimmersion and waited for a sign from Jeremy that he was ready to go the next step and the next and finally invite a child his own age into the house. When, after a while, we began to host an occasional neighbor or a schoolmate, we managed that with the same philosophy—structured the playtime with arts, crafts, puzzles, games, outings so that the experience could be successful all around. Our goal was to help Jeremy see that friendship was worth it and to stir up a positive experience for the visiting child so that he would naturally want to come back. Sometimes this worked. Sometimes it didn't. No matter what, Jeremy and I would sit quietly in the session's aftermath and explore our feelings, together investigate social concepts such as collaboration, alienation, manipulation, and deception.

Over time, Jeremy's acquisition of language opened a window onto his world. No more did he merely arrange the objects of his obsessions on the carpeted floor or the asphalt driveway. He indulged us in their mysteries, expressed his opinions, divulged his special knowledge, invited us to see the plane, the train, the car as he did. My husband excelled at escaping into Jeremy's labyrinthine worlds—could follow the rules of the hand-drawn traffic signs, drop the right bombs from the right bombing aircraft, switch the trains from track to appropriate track. He could rebuild a broken Lego construction because he understood the intent behind

Jeremy's design. Could remove a car from the splendid sequence of cars because Jeremy trusted him to properly reinsert it. Could make Jeremy laugh, engage him in some healthy verbal sparring, and even though I wasn't nearly as good as my husband was at all of this, didn't have the precision of memory demanded by my young son's ingenuity, I did get better at learning how to stop fearing the passions that consumed him. I learned to see them differently. Learned to understand that the obsessions provided an opportunity to let the language out. Learned how to pull Jeremy *through* the obsession instead of yanking him straight *out* of it, how to stretch him bit by bit from compulsion toward conversation. Not surprisingly, Jeremy was most fluid when speaking about the things he profoundly loved, and after a long, long time I learned to let him practice this fluidity, not to shut it off like a faucet. We got better at balance, I guess I'm saying. I gave Jeremy more room to grow into himself. This he reciprocated many times over by unwinding more of his spool of silk thread—stroking my hair at the end of the day, sharing his dreams in the night's deep dark, running down the hall just to say that he loved me. *Hey, I love you, too,* I'd tell him, reaching for him, pulling him up in my arms, collecting my hot emotion above the pillow of his hair before I'd let him back down to the floor. Because how could he possibly, at his age, comprehend how much his words meant to his mother?

In time—and it did take a while, it did—I got to understand Jeremy's pacing: his habit of trotting up and down the hallway, or back and forth in the front yard, leaving the indelible impression of his footprints. This understanding arose not out of something I analytically determined but out of the words Jeremy himself finally deployed, *I'm playing movies in my mind, and I need to walk or the movies aren't there.* What did he mean? I didn't know at first, but because he had at last put forth an explanation, I could respect it and leverage it, begin to ask him questions about what he saw in his mind. When it became clear to him that I was genuine in my desire to understand, I was rewarded: he let me further into his world. We learned together that he needed thirty minutes, no more, to run a movie in his mind. We struck a deal that gave him that half hour at home, once each day. I promised not to interrupt if he promised to play with me later, and things worked out okay. We made progress in the house, and one day, lying beside Jeremy with a book in my hand, I came upon a shock of words by the extraordinarily talented autistic woman Temple Grandin: *I store information in my head as if it were on a CD-ROM disc. When I recall something I have learned, I replay the video in my mind. The videos in my memory are always specific.* My God. I sat up. My God. "Hey, Jeremy," I called to him. "Is it like this for you?" I read him Grandin's first words. I read him other passages of hers, too. He listened carefully, then smiled broadly and looked at me through the wells of his eyes. "Of course," he answered emphatically. "I already told you. I play real movies in my mind." Talking with Jeremy about the way his mind works became another port of entry. It became some of the most satisfying conversation I will ever have, one of the many privileges I have as a mother to my son.

I DO NOT believe that my husband and I have healed our child. We do not even know what normal is, what finished looks like, what neurological and environmental hurdles we are still facing. We don't know what could have been done that wasn't, what shouldn't have been done that was. The only truth we have in our house today is that we have given our son the room to heal himself—a safe place, the right friends, information, conversation, a buffer from the world when he needs that buffer. We have learned to look for schools and camps and therapists that see the issues the way we do; for people and institutions that understand that kindness is the deepest cure, that there is always room for hope. We have appreciated, more than words will ever say, those who have loved Jeremy for who he is and those who have—simply out of the goodness of their hearts—made room for him in a classroom, come to his rescue at recess, carried him up on their shoulders, curled his fingers around a pencil, divulged the secret of basketball, invited him over to play. Jeremy has responded to kindness, and how surprising can this be? He's just human, like the rest of us. Carving out his place upon this planet.

For every child that leaves a doctor's office with a not otherwise specified pervasive developmental disorder, the particulars are going to be different. I know of a little "PDD" boy who two years ago had no words at all; today he's telling his aunt how much he loves her. I know of a little girl who's the swimming champion of her pool club. I know of another boy who has a church full of friends, hundreds of people he can count on. I know of yet another little boy who is learning to look his father in the eyes. The books don't say what to do with children like these because in the end they cannot: ultimately these children are individuals. Like all children, they test the canons of parenting. But the books also don't do as much as they might when it comes to sending a message about love. It counts. It counts enormously. It leads us out of the valley and toward the hills.

Several weeks ago, I was standing in Jeremy's school

yard, fighting the sadness and frustration that still sometimes comes. Jeremy had been in a down cycle, and he was
struggling during recess, not willing to play, consumed by
mind movies, alienating himself from friends who were
trying to reach him. I had just dropped Jeremy off and I
was virtually alone, studying the playground, picturing
Jeremy running along the edges there, trying to understand
what I should do. Saunders was nearby, and he finally
approached me, pulled on his beard, and said, a farmer's
great wisdom, "Ma'am, I've got a story to tell you."

"What's that?" I asked, not sure I had the wherewithal to
hear him out.

"Well, there was a boy," he began, "a boy like Jeremy
when I was growing up."

"There was?" I asked, thinking it was odd, one doesn't
hear much about this sort of thing in other generations.

"Yes, ma'am," Saunders continued. "There was a boy
like that, ran around the rim of playgrounds, didn't go in
very much for school-yard games. I recall, I do, him talking
about movies in his mind, and I recall that he was a quiet
boy, real intelligent, but on the outside, always. Well, that
boy, ma'am, I reckon he's about my age right now. And last
I heard, he was an ambassador somewhere. Married. Big
house. Two great kids. Things fall away, ma'am. I believe
they do. You just can't stop looking ahead."

palsy

*L*ater, two children will dance. Others, raggedly arranged in the humid auditorium, will hula, sway, smile recklessly, clap, but only two children will dance. Wearing electric wheels for legs, they will draw arcs across the floor and open and close their own parentheses. They will do-si and -do, their stemlike necks bending with each change in direction. He will breathe from a shallow place and bow. She will put one thread of a finger into the air and spin, and spin, and this is the center of the story, this is its heart: the grace of palsy in an afternoon dance.

⟞

WE DO NOT expect what we find. We arrive with our own purpose and preoccupations, and we come early; it is that kind of show. Everyone assembled here in the wood-floored, white-walled auditorium is tied by an invisible string to a child backstage, and there is an order to things, the familiar courtesies of strangers. I have come with my mother. I have come for my son. He turns seven today, a lucky number.

Back there somewhere, Jeremy is rehearsing with his tribe: a little hula, a little shuffle, a little moment for the stage. Who would have thought it? Who would have guessed it five years ago, when we received the diagnosis? In the simmering noise of the crowd, my thoughts slide and slide backward, then pull themselves forward; occasionally, I speak to my mother. "It's crowded," I say. "I know that person," I say, pointing. "See the redhead? She drives a hot-pink Seville." It's noise between my thoughts, and it's making me dizzy, but I feel that I owe my mother a brush of conversation, and this is all that I have in me today. "Mom," I finally confide. "About Jeremy . . ." I begin. And my mother says, "Please. Please. He'll be fine."

I know that he will be. I know that he is. Jeremy is fine now, but life is fragile, and who can make predictions about what will happen when a curtain is drawn—when the velvet pulls away and the child, now reaching seven, appears at last upon the stage. "There are a lot of people here, Mom," I say. I worry about Jeremy and his fear of crowds. "What matters is that Jeremy's here," my mother answers. Everything else is extra.

The room fills. Seated in the front row, we feel the pressure building behind us. We are aware of movement on the periphery, of mothers sitting against the walls because there are now no chairs, of ladies' skirts drawn tight as tents across the knobs of knees. We are aware of cameras being bolted to their tripods, of siblings getting out of hand, of society knitting itself into a warm plaid fabric. "Mom," I say. "What if he can't do it? Or what if he can, and won't?" "He has always come through," my mother says, and then she fans her face with the Hula Dance program.

It is true, I think. At every fork in Jeremy's journey, he has made a choice, and he's pulled through. Acquiring speech. Acquiring strength. Acquiring rhythm. Acquiring access. Freeing his heart through his words—simple phrases without which I would not have survived: *I love you, Mommy. How are you, Mommy? Did you do anything special today?*

We are aware of hushing. We are aware of one young adult male slopping around in flip-flops as he moves between the unclipped hedges of the center aisle and toward the clearing up front. His Hawaiian shirt is neon green and desperate yellow. The piece of gold in his left ear is a hoop. The little girl at his side stands as tall as his shoulder, wearing a well-wrapped pink sheet that explodes—we hear it popping—with the catalytic fire of bright white threads. As if to guard them from the bulging audience, a phalanx of square-shouldered counselors now arrive—strong young women who convey, by their gestures, that anything is possible. She muscles the lights. She commands the canned music. She uncrumples a list from her fist and points a finger. She gestures boldly with her hands and her hands become mops, and without ever touching the overflowing floor, she has managed the spills: toes, cameras, babies all retract.

One is aware of this. One knows that now, during the final preparations for the Hula Dance extravaganza, we—the audience, the parents, the siblings, the glass-eyed cameras, my mother, myself—must release ourselves into the care of counselors and children. The room begins to slouch like a wave being turned back to sea. I lose my equilibrium, and when I close my eyes, I see that my mind is busy separating itself into angular shades of gray. It's the beginning of a migraine, and I have never been able to explain it, but at times like these, it happens.

The truth is that I can no longer explain most things, nor can I make them any better with my words. How haunting this is: for a writer, for a mother, for a person in the world. *Jeremy*, I have said more times than one could count, *I love you. I love you. You fill my heart.* But there is nothing in those words about the way I deeply feel. About how Jeremy has taken me through these last seven years of life and taught me wonder. He has completed me—wrenched me in and out of myself, forced me past my boundaries, looked into me with his wide chocolate eyes, and demanded loyalty, spirituality, and faith. *I'm not letting you down*, he has proven over and over, and he has elevated me so that I can stand and look up and see who he is and who I must somehow be, to be his mother. I cannot explain this. I cannot put language around it, but Jeremy, with his tinge of disability and his one gigantic heart, has brought me here, today, where I sit beside my mother, loving my son so absolutely and speechlessly, and still, still afraid of what will happen on the stage.

Behind me, I sense the room breathing and humming. I know that the curtain will soon rise, and I know that when I open my eyes I will no longer see the gray angles of my migraine, but crisp, jagging flashes of hot pain instead. I will focus my vision after that, and hold one hand over my left eye so that the stage will come into view. But for now I remain in the space of gray angles. My mind bobs on the surface of itself; there are collisions. Somewhere outside this gray, my mother is sitting, fanning herself with the Hula Dance program, and I would like to reach her with words, but it's impossible. The only stories that come to mind are stories about other mothers, conversations I've had. Frozen moments when I have, for example, stood in a neighbor's backyard, and stood, and helplessly listened to a sadness that slowly formed itself in words. "Two babies," this neighbor told me. "Two boys. Two children that I carry here, inside of me. And one will live and one, a genetic complication, will not. And what I want," this neighbor told me, "and what I want, I really want, is to hold both babies in my arms and bring them home and to tell them, for all of time, how much they're loved." *Words,* she said, *I will give my two sons words. For as long as God will keep them on this earth.*

Now the noise in the room is less than the silence. I open one eye and see that the capable counselors are crouched on the floor and the parents with the cameras are poised to film. Even the siblings have been brought into line, and the young man and the little girl at the front of the room exchange a few final, whispered vows in anticipation of the curtain that will soon lift from the ground. "They're getting ready to go," my mother leans over to tell me, and I draw in one long, arrhythmic breath, and slouch, at last, into my nubby plastic chair.

"Ladies and gentlemen," the little girl begins. "We are so pleased that you have come to see our show."

"It's full of talent," the young man answers. "It's full of stars."

"And we would not be here today," the little girl tells us, "were it not for the hard work of the Day Camp youngsters."

"Who have been practicing all week . . ."

"Who have made their very own costumes . . ."

"So sit back."

"You must relax."

"Listen closely for the sound of congo drums."

The audience rises to attention, and now we all lean out of our slouches and fall forward, toward the stage—my hand on my eye, my mother's program in her lap. A tinny, one-speaker version of a calypso song jiggles through the atmosphere and begins to rock the room. The young man and the child announcer step aside, encourage all eyes forward. The curtain begins its creak to heaven, and all anyone can see at first is the tiny sneakers and the knotted socks and the sometimes sandals; there's a hint of painted toes. There are forty feet on the stage and some are better clad than others, and some are tapping, and some are still rehearsing the shuffle right, the shuffle left, the tap the toes, the jump, the smack, smack, smack, the swivel on the heels.

And the Belafonte impostor is now singing the chorus, and the curtain keeps ascending, and twenty happy, anxious pairs of feet crook and stomp, and now we the audience make acquaintance with the props: floppy paper fish that curl beneath the weight of excess poster paint; hairy cardboard palm trees, their colors drying; a boat that's bobbing buoyesque; a dozen plastic leis strewn like confetti on the floor. We've been transported. We clap. We roar. Bolt upright now in our plastic chairs, we connect ankles to knees to twisted hips to glossy faces. The wheeze and pop of exultation goes off around the room like camera lights.

In their ragged line, the children torque their way forward, arms punched to the left, to the right, chins deliberately wagging, rhythms far exceeding whatever this Belafonte mimic can deliver. This is the show, and we wag with it, taking our direction from the children, too bungled by noise and atmosphere to begin to break the whole into its parts. "Mom?" I half whisper, half scream. "Do you see him?" But it's too late to ask or answer that question, because now, halfway between the nether of the background and the edge of the sea, the children hush one another and, remembering something, suddenly, expectantly, stare off into the wings. Our eyes follow their eyes, take their cue.

They come from opposite directions—the girl and the boy in their chairs. Her gold hair susurrates around her face. His eyes, two pools of dark liquid, are as huge and as gentle as a fawn's. Their skin is the same unnameable aspect of white, and everything is loose and fragile about them but their hands, their fingers, which cling to the controls of their chairs and propel their bodies across the stage. It is enough for us that these children have appeared, but now they begin to dance, whirring in and out of each other's paths like bright tropical birds. I need both of my eyes to see this, and I bring my hand to my lap, but still it is a mystery, it is beyond human, how these two children in their crumple of bones glide and circle each other and spin, their wheels making no noises as they turn, their faces shy, soft as feathers, and triumphant.

We do not speak to one another. We do not lean over and say, *But they are tiny. But they are fragile.* We only watch them, and now we lift our eyes and watch the twenty who stand behind the two children on wheels, the twenty, Jeremy among them, who are upright as props and smiling, beaming, proud of all they can do, of who they can be on that stage—despite genetics, despite diagnoses, despite haphazard labels, despite whatever legacies their swaying shoulders bear. We, here in our plastic chairs, cannot reach out and we cannot touch; it is impossible to hold on to this beauty. We are forced to sit and to see that life is sacred and secret, and we are forced to understand these things without the tendril of touch or the logic of words. We are elevated to the courage of mothers and of fathers, to the courage of children everywhere.

last rights

*M*ommy, *I know what's going to happen when I grow up.*

What's that?

I'm going to drive to the church and get a wife.

Okay.

Then my wife and me will drive to the hospital and pick up our kid.

A kid?

Yup. A boy with my same hairstyle.

And after that, what?

I'll take my kid and my wife to the house that I live in and then I'll go to work in my rouge-red Wrangler.

What will you do?

Four jobs: work at Jeep Eagle, be a baker, sing in a band with my friends from school, and mostly, all the time, be a daddy.

Sounds just right. But will you ever come and visit?

Of course.

Will you let me hold the boy that looks like you?

Of course. You'll be the grandmom because you'll have white hair. You'll be really old when I'm grown up.

acknowledgments

I wish to thank: My husband, Bill, a gentle spirit, who endured, forgave, and offered wisdom, time, and love.

Andrée Seu, who read most every word, commented brilliantly, and was—despite the weather we were having—a constant source of light.

Amy Rennert, a gift from above, an agent with integrity, a friend.

Alane Salierno Mason, who knew just what to say and when to say it, and put her heart right at the center of this book.

My extended family and my friends, all of whom are Jeremy's friends, too, and indispensable.

My parents, Jeremy's grandmom and grandpop, who were there for Jeremy from the start, invoking joy.

A Slant of Sun is the story of one child's triumph over a particular set of challenges. Many organizations exist today to help parents sort through the therapeutic options and possibilities best suited for their own children. For an overview listing of helpful Internet sites, please contact the following website:

http://www.pov3.com/slant.html